# 110 Life Skills for

# Teenage Boys

From Basic Survival Skills to Adulting Like a Pro.
Your Ultimate Guide to Building Unbreakable
Confidence in Yourself

**Tory Hunt**

# TABLE OF CONTENT

# Introduction

D id you know that being a teenager today comes with its own set of unique challenges? You are not alone. Many teenagers face these challenges, from dealing with anxiety and social media to wanting to become more independent.

Here's a reality check for you:

- 89% say life would have been easier had they learned practical skills.
- For the first time since the Great Depression, over half of young adults live with their parents.
- 83% of teenagers lack financial management skills.

- Anxiety disorders affect about one-third of all adolescents ages 13 to 18.
- A recent poll found that 81% of recent college graduates wish they had learned more practical skills in school.
- Roughly 30% of recent graduates can't receive a credit card, loan, or place to live because they need a higher credit score.
- More than a quarter of Gen Z can't bake a cake from a mix.

Right now, you might be worried about becoming a responsible adult and handling life on your own without your parents' guidance. Nobody wants to move back in with their parents simply because they can't handle being independent, right?

But guess what? You don't have to face these challenges alone. "110 Life Skills for Teenage Boys" is here to lend a helping hand. This guide isn't your typical boring manual; it's here to make learning and growing as easy as pie. You will get to know yourself better, appreciate your unique qualities, and build stronger relationships with others.

As a teenager, you're probably super busy, and sometimes it's hard to figure out where to start when becoming an adult. Well, this guide is the perfect starting point. You'll learn all the skills you need to tackle the challenges that come your way and set yourself up for success as you journey into adulthood.

In years to come, you'll experience much growth and change. The teen years are full of promise and peril. This is the time when most people begin making plans for adulthood. As you enter maturity, now is the moment to lay the groundwork for your future. You'll soon be making crucial choices that determine your future.

The real issue is how well-prepare you are for the next step in your life journey. Once you make wise choices, you may see every experience as a chance to learn something new. Plus you grow up and learn to be responsible adult thanks to the lesson you've learned.

You see, the choices you make now will shape your future. So, are you ready to face it head-on? Don't worry if you are not there yet. We all learn and grow at our own pace. Just remember, life skills are like any other; they take time and practice.

While traditional education is valuable, real-life experiences can teach you things school doesn't cover. As you grow older, you will face more responsibilities and the need to acquire practical life skills. That's where "110 Life Skills for Teenage Boys" comes into play. This book can help you tackle daily challenges, become self-sufficient, and balance all aspects of your life.

Although the internet provides access to a lot of information, it can be daunting to sift through it all and find the specific pieces of data that will be most useful to you. And sorting through what's true and what isn't may be a real pain. In addition, while you can certainly learn a lot from your parents or other close relatives, they may be unable to provide guidance in some crucial areas. This manual provides a comprehensive road map that may be used to lay the groundwork for the kind of future that has always been a source of inspiration for you.

When you finish reading this book, you will have the tools and knowledge you need to face any challenges that come your way. Whether you are still in school, finishing up high school, heading off to college, or have already found yourself in the real world, it's never too late to learn these 110 life skills to help you succeed. Okay, so let's begin!

# Chapter 1

## Prioritizing Your Well-Being

Meet Jimmy, a regular teenage guy like you who starts developing facial hair earlier than his buddies. He likes feeling unique and cool, so he wasn't keen on shaving and losing his standout feature. Even though his dad told him that saving could make his facial hair grow better, he brushed it off. But then, here comes his crush, Sarah, casually mentioning his wispy mustache. It was like a wake-up call. Jimmy realized it might be time to step up his grooming game.

In this chapter, we dive into self-care and start with Jimmy's story. Self-care is not just about looking good; it's about personal hygiene, grooming habits, and mental and emotional well-being. By mastering these essential skills, you can boost your confidence, well-being, and overall success in life.

Throughout this chapter, we will cover crucial topics that every teenage boy should know, including safe shaving techniques, treating razor burn, selecting the right deodorant, hair care tips, maintaining fresh breath, skincare routines, nail and foot care, and the significance of self-care activities.

By embracing these life skills, you can improve your physical appearance, develop self-confidence, present yourself with pride, and make a positive impression on others. Remember that self-care is about grooming, prioritizing your well-being, and nurturing your growth as an independent teenage boy.

So, let's begin this self-care journey together.

# Life Skill #1: Know How to Shave

If you're thinking about shaving for the first time, it's best to talk with a trusted adult like your dad or older sibling who already shaves. They can help you determine if you're ready to begin. Typically, you'll notice it's time to start shaving when your chin and upper lip hair get longer and darker.

**Choosing the Right Razor**

You should look for a razor that fits your needs and is safe to use. Find an adult, like a parent or an older brother, to take you shopping. You can choose from electric or disposable razors. Here's a bit more detail about each:

- **Electric razors.** It's easy to travel with an electric razor. Yet, many razors do not provide a close shave like disposable ones. Choose an electric razor with pivoting heads so it can follow the shape of your face. Some electric razors release lubricants as you shave to better care for your skin. But even an electric razor has the potential to cause skin irritation. Spend some time looking before committing to one.
- **Disposable razors.** If you choose a disposable razor, you must prep your face with shaving cream or gel. You can protect your face from nicks and cuts by using one of these face creams or gels. Many lotions and gels are available. Some have vitamins and moisturizers to keep your face from getting too dry. Try different face creams and gels to find what suits you best, especially if your skin is sensitive.

## Shaving Process

Before you start shaving, ensure you have all the necessary supplies, such as  a sharp razor, shaving cream or gel, aftershave or moisturizer.  Begin by wetting your skin and hair with warm water to soften them before shaving.  Apply shaving cream or gel next to aid in softening.  When you are ready, shaving in the same direction that your hair grows is essential to minimize irritation.  Clean the blade after each stroke to remove excess hair and shaving cream.  Rinse your face with cold water to close the pores after shaving, and gently pat your face dry after rinsing. Finally, store your razor in a dry place.

If you're new to shaving, starting with disposable razors is best to minimize the chances of accidentally cutting yourself. As you become more proficient, you'll feel more comfortable and confident. Just remember to go slowly and follow the proper steps.

# Life Skill #2: Understanding Dry Shaving vs. Wet Shaving

There are different methods available when it comes to shaving. As a beginner, you might be confused. Let's discuss them.

Which type of shave is better for me, wet or dry? First, let's learn the differences.

**What is Wet Shaving?**

In the first step of wet shaving, hot water is used to soften facial hair and open pores so that the shaving can go more smoothly. In this time-tested way to get rid of facial hair, a sharp razor is brought close to the skin at the spot where the hair needs to be cut. A wet shaving kit usually has shaving cream, a cartridge razor with one or more blades, and a shaving brush.

**What is Dry Shaving?**

A dry shave, which requires an electric razor, is a relatively recent development. A foil electric shaver can shave through wet or dry facial hair, so there's no need to worry about lathering up before use.

The advantages and disadvantages of each shaving technique are different. If you have sensitive skin, don't want to spend too much time in the bathroom, and want a close shave, then a dry shave might be better than a wet one. Wet shaving is best for closeness and comfort, although dry shaving can save time and allow you to shave in either direction. You need to invest in a good shaver if you have sensitive skin and often have red, irritated patches after shaving. As there are fewer blades in an electric shaver, there is less pulling on the skin of the face.

## Life Skill #3: How to Treat Razor Burn

If you are new to shaving, you may encounter a common issue, like razor burn. Don't worry; there are ways to treat it. Let's explore some options.

## What Causes Razor Burn?

Razor burn occurs when a razor blade irritates the skin and hair follicles. It is painful and could make you sick. Tenderness and swelling, itchiness, bruising or stinging sensations, and pain are all signs of razor burn. Checking the razor blade, the shaver's skill, and the medicine cabinet will help you avoid razor burn. An old, dull blade may be the cause of a shaving rash. Softening the hair and skin with a moisturizer or soap before shaving is essential.

## How to Treat Razor Burns

While razor burn heals on its own in most cases, there are ways to ease the discomfort in the meantime.

- Apply a cool, damp compress for up to 20 minutes, as often as needed.
- Use natural astringent liquids like apple cider vinegar, tea tree oil, chilled black tea, and witch hazel extract to reduce inflammation and redness.
- Use natural oils like avocado, olive, coconut, and sweet almond oil to soothe and relieve itching, pain, and burning.
- Apply aloe vera gel directly from the plant or buy it from a store for sensitive or damaged skin.
- You can also find over-the-counter lotions like aftershave, baby products, hydrocortisone, salicylic

acid, and razor bump treatments at drugstores and grocery stores.

## Life Skill #4: Picking the Right Deodorant

Selecting the right deodorant is important because not all of them are the same. There are two main types to consider: deodorant and antiperspirant. Which one is best for you?

**Antiperspirant**: Antiperspirant works as a deodorant, but its aluminum-based ingredients clog the pores in the armpits, stopping sweat from coming out. This can cause yellow pit stains and irritation.

**Deodorant**: Deodorant helps mask the smell when you start sweating by targeting the bacteria that cause it. This is a healthier option, as your body needs to sweat to eliminate toxins.

Deodorant is optimal for normal sweat and odor, while antiperspirant is optimal for excessive sweat and foul odor. Deodorant is healthier, while antiperspirant is better for sensitive skin.

**Why You Should Switch to an All-Natural Deodorant Instead of a Chemical One**

**Natural deodorant**: Natural deodorants use natural ingredients to get rid of odors while letting sweat do its natural job of getting rid of toxins and chemicals.

**Chemical deodorant**: Many deodorants in the market contain toxic chemicals like aluminum and perfumes, which can be harmful. Even budget-friendly deodorants often have these harmful chemicals and scents to keep their prices low. Finding a good all-natural deodorant that is safe for your skin is essential. The best natural deodorants include coconut oil, shea butter, tapioca starch, caprylic triglyceride, castor seed oil, sunflower seed oil, and ozokerite.

## Life Skill #5: Don't Forget Hair Care

Maintaining healthy and well-groomed hair is important for a polished look. Regular hair care prevents damage and ensures your hair is neat and stylish. Start by getting a haircut every 6-8 weeks to maintain its health and avoid those pesky split ends. Depending on your hair type and oiliness, wash your hair regularly with a mild shampoo, 2-3 times per week. After shampooing, always apply conditioner for an extra boost of moisture.

Rinse with lukewarm or cool water to preserve the natural oils. Hot water can strip them away, leading to dryness.

When drying, pat your hair gently with a towel to remove excess moisture, avoiding vigorous rubbing to prevent frizz and damage. Limit heat styling tools, opt for a wattage hair dryer with a power level under 1200 watts, and protect your hair from the sun with a hat or leave-in conditioner with UV protection.

Don't let swimming in a chlorine-filled pool or the elements harm your hair. Consider using a swim cap or leave-in conditioner for added protection. Avoid running fingers through hair too often to prevent the transfer of oils from hands to hair, causing greasiness. Combat dandruff promptly with pH-balanced shampoos, or try a few drops of vinegar or lemon in your rinse water.

Choose a brush or comb with rounded teeth, and brush damp hair gently to prevent damage. Keep your tools clean, and remember, a balanced diet with proper nutrients and sufficient water intake contributes to healthy hair growth. Caring for your hair is a simple yet effective way to showcase your best self.

## Life Skill #6: Fresh Breath, Fresh You

If you're concerned about how others perceive you, taking care of your oral hygiene is essential. Bad breath can be a real deal-breaker, so prioritize it!

What steps can you take to avoid bad breath? Here are some ways to stop or reduce it:

- Brush and floss more regularly.
- Gargle with water.
- Use a tongue scraper.
- Steer clear of foods that cause bad breath.
- Instead of mints, eat gum after supper.
- Maintain healthy gums.
- Moisten your mouth.
- Keep your dental devices clean.
- See your dentist routinely, at least twice a year.
- Quit smoking cigarettes and chewing tobacco.
- Consume more fruits and vegetables while consuming less meat.
- Maintain a record of the items you eat.

## Life Skill #7: Healthy Skin, Happy You

Taking care of your skin is not just for the ladies. With all the environmental pollution, our skin needs all the protection it can get. Here are four super simple steps that will leave your skin looking great:

**Cleanse**: Wash your face daily to maintain clear and healthy skin, preventing acne by removing dirt, oil, and dead skin cells, oil, and dead skin.

1. **Hydrate or Moisturize**: Water, oil, or a combination of the two can be used to rehydrate the skin.

2. **Treat**: Acne occurs when the skin pores become blocked, a prevalent issue among teenagers. While soaps and astringents can help reduce oiliness, they do not affect the body's natural sebum production. Scrubbing the skin can irritate, so it should be avoided. Using benzoyl peroxide products sparingly, once a day in the evening, can help with mild acne. Treating the entire oily face, including the forehead, chin, nose, and cheeks, rather than just the breakout areas is essential.

3. **Protect**: Always remember to apply sunscreen after washing your face in the morning. Always protect your skin from harmful UV rays, both during the day and at night, with a moisturizing sunscreen that contains zinc oxide (at least 7%) and an SPF of 30 or higher, tailored to your skin tone.

## Life Skill #8: Nail It!

People notice your nails more than you think! Having clean and well-groomed nails isn't just for shows. It's about hygiene and self-care. Neglecting them can give the impression that you don't value yourself.

## 1. Trim Your Nails After a Shower

The best time to trim your fingernails is after a revitalizing shower. Warm water helps remove calluses and tidy up cuticles while softening the nails, making trimming and shaping them easier.

## 2. Take Care While Trimming Your Nails

To trim your nails, use nail clippers and follow their natural shape. It's important to avoid cutting them too short, as it can cause discomfort and ingrown nails. Make clean cuts from beginning to end to prevent jagged edges.

## 3. File Your Fingernails Down

You can use a nail file to round off the corners of your nails. A nail file can be used to give your nails the desired form.

## 4. The Proper Method for Removing Hangnails

You could seriously injure yourself if you try to remove your hangnails. If you must get rid of them, use a clipper. Don't yank on hangnails; you could hurt the nail's inner structure and the skin underneath.

# Life Skill #9: Don't Neglect Your Feet

Taking good care of your feet is vital beyond just wearing shoes and sandals. Here are some helpful tips for maintaining healthy feet:

- Put on clean socks daily. Changing your socks once or twice a day will help keep your feet dry and comfortable throughout the day.
- Use some soap and water to clean your feet. Those who want to avoid or control foot-related ailments should wash their feet with soap and water daily.
- Get your feet completely dry. The spaces between your toes require special attention while drying your feet after a bath or shower. The lotion is fine to use.
- Trim toenails with a clean, diagonal cut. Cut your toenails short and sterilize the clipper with some rubbing alcohol. Avoid attempting a one-step nail trim or digging at the sides of your toenails. Just make a clean cut, allowing the nails to grow out slightly.
- Don't try to solve an issue by hacking at your foot. Calluses can be treated with a pumice stone or by adding extra padding to your shoes instead of cutting off bits of your flesh.

# Life Skill #10: Don't Forget Self-Care

Taking care of yourself is super important, especially for teenage boys. Making self-care practices a regular part of your routine will make you feel physically and mentally better. Plus, it's a great way to establish positive habits and live a happier life overall. So remember to prioritize self-care and make it a regular part of your life! Here are some self-care ideas for you:

## Exercising

Exercise is a terrific way to take care of yourself. Endorphins are substances released by the body after exercise that have been shown to improve mood. You can exercise on your own time and reap the benefits by running, jogging, walking, swimming, or riding a bike.

## Spending Time with Friends and Family

Being among others that boost your confidence is a great way to spend time. Make plans to hang out with the individuals you enjoy being with and do things you want to do.

## Practicing Yoga and Meditation

Yoga and meditation are wonderful methods for focusing inward attention on one's body and mind. You may discover many videos on YouTube that will walk you through your first practice or meditation if you need help figuring out where to start.

## Cooking

Self-care activities like cooking can be really beneficial. Spending time in the kitchen may be relaxing, whether alone or with loved ones.

## Playing or Listening to Music

Spending time alone learning music or performing an instrument can be very rewarding. Setting the goal of learning a specific song can be a mentally stimulating and relaxing way to spend time alone.

## Reading

Reading is a great form of self-care since it forces readers to relax and focus on themselves rather than the world around them. Reading is a great opportunity to escape from the stresses and cares of everyday life and experience a new and exciting world via your imagination.

## Taking a Bath or Shower

Taking a bath is a terrific way to care of yourself and unwind. Even if you don't have a bathtub, a long shower can be a relaxing way to give yourself time and space.

## Organizing Your Space

Taking the effort to clean and organize your personal space (such as your workspace or bedroom) is a terrific act of self-care since it allows you to declutter your mind while producing a pleasant environment to spend time in.

Remember, taking care of yourself is essential, not just for your looks but also for your mental and emotional health. By practicing self-care, you can focus on personal growth, happiness, and confidence. Make self-care a priority in your routine for better health and happiness. You deserve it!

# Chapter 2

## Keep Yourself Looking Stylish

I f you're like Fred and want to improve your fashion game, this chapter is for you! He struggled with wrinkled dress shirts and creased slacks, which made him feel frustrated and stressed when attending formal events. But don't worry, we have some tips and techniques to help you maintain a stylish appearance and leave a lasting impression. Let's get started!

## Life skill #11: Suit Up in Style

When you're young, buying a suit can be a big deal. Let's talk about how you can select the perfect suit for yourself, ensuring that you'll have the best one when you need it in the future.

1. **Set Your Budget:** Determine your budget and aim to spend between $200 and $2,000 on your first suit.

2. **Choose Your Fabric:** Choose  suit made of 100% wool if you can afford it, but be aware that wool blends are also available at a lower cost. Over the $500-$1000 price range, you may expect to find only 100% wool options.

3. **Fit Is Key:**  If you're not sure if the suit can be altered, don't buy it if it doesn't fit. Be sure to check the following:

## Suit jacket shoulders

If the shoulders don't line up with your natural shoulder line, you shouldn't buy the suit. Jacket shoulder adjustments are as complex and expensive.

## Suit jacket chest size

In general, a jacket is too large if you can fit two fists into the front of it. Tailoring can take off up to two inches without affecting the proportions or the aesthetics of the jacket or its pockets.

## Suit jacket length

Stow your arms neatly at your sides. The jacket's hemline ought to reach approximately the knuckles. Your jacket should reach down to cover your buttocks at the back. That's about the maximum length or minimum length it should be.

4. **Buy the Right Dress Shirt:** Dress shirts can be any shade of light blue, pink, or lavender, but traditional white is always appropriate.

5. **Match Your Suit and Shoes:** A black Balmoral Oxford is the quintessential shoe to complement any suit. The closed-lacing method of an Oxford shoe makes it the most formal option.

6. **Choose Your Neckwear:** Neckwear is a standard component of a business outfit. It's the finishing touch on the dress. Red is generally considered a fail-safe hue unless it's a vibrant shade. Purple, the color of monarchs, is another option, along with dark blue and green.

## Life Skill #12: Folding Your Shirts

Folding a shirt may seem small, but it isn't. Knowing how to fold a shirt will give you satisfaction. It not only prevents wrinkles but also helps with organization. Here are some steps to follow when folding different types of shirts:

### Folding a T-Shirt

1. Spread out your T-shirt so that the front is facing up.
2. To do this, fold the short sleeve back in one direction and then the other. Flip it over and do it again.

3. Shirts can be folded into a rectangle by bringing the collar down to the hem.
4. Do another half-fold with the shirt. If the shirt is particularly lengthy, you may need to fold it into thirds.
5. Keep the T-shirt hanging when folded.

## Folding a Dress Shirt

1. Make sure the shirt is buttoned and flat by laying it flat.

2. Tuck the sleeves into the shirt's middle.

3. Cross the cuffs of both sleeves over the center of your back by folding them horizontally. The side seams of the garment should not be creased.

4. Make a V at the collar by folding the shirt's side seams equally from shoulder to hem,

5. Then folding the sleeves again to meet in the center. Further down the shirt, the sides may or may not touch.

6. Split it in half horizontally. Using two hands at the shirt's hem, fold it in half vertically from the bottom up until the hem meets the base of the collar.

7. You may need to do this once or twice, depending on the depth of your closet.

8. Turn the shirt inside out before putting it away.

# Life Skill #13: Irons are Your Friend

If you're not confident in your ironing abilities, don't worry. By mastering this simple skill, you can easily maintain your clothes without relying on others.

**Iron a Dress Shirt**

1. Start with the collar:
    - The interior of the collar needs to be starched and pressed from end to end.
    - Simply reverse the garment and repeat the process to finish the outside of collar
2. Shift to the Shoulders:
    - Starch and press the shirt's yoke (the part right below the collar).
3. Move to the cuffs:
    - Unbutton all the buttons on one sleeve and lay it flat on the ironing board.
    - Press with starch from edge to edge, avoiding the buttons.
    - The cuff should be turned inside out, and repeat the process.
    - Do this method on the other cuffs.
4. Iron the sleeves:
    - Start by smoothing both layers when starching and pressing.

- Place the seam at the bottom of the sleeve. Iron from top to bottom, avoiding the outer edge.
- Press the edge while working your way down to avoid unwanted creases.

5. Iron on the back:
   - Spread the shirt out on the ironing board to allow the shoulders to lay flat.
   - Apply the starch gradually, starting at the top to the bottom.

6. Focus on the front:
   - Start ironing the button side, use the starch spray and gently press in the spaces between the button sets.
   - Avoid iron over a button.
   - Methodically move down from the top of the shirt.

7. Polish up the placket:
   - Both the front and back of the buttonhole placket should be ironed on the reverse side of the shirt.

## Life Skill #14: Get Rid of Those Stains

Here are some tips for removing common stains and keeping your clothes clean and presentable.

## Ink Stains

Using a cotton swab dipped in clear rubbing alcohol, carefully work your way in from the edge of the stain, changing swabs as they get dirty.

## Grease Stains

1. Mix vinegar and water in equal parts and apply generously.
2. Then wash it with detergent and water.
3. Checked to ensure the stain is gone before drying it.

## Pet Urine Stains and Smells

1. Wash an item in hot water with strong detergents .
2. Add one cup of white distilled vinegar to the rinse water.
3. For old stains and strong odors, make a solution of cool water and two cups of white vinegar and soak the fabric overnight.
4. Dry the item outside on a clothesline to help eliminate odors.

## Mud Stains

1. Soak the affected area in water.

2. Scrub the stain with laundry soap and a brush, repeating the process if necessary for particularly tough stains.

**Grass Stains**

1. Apply stain remover or regular laundry detergent to the affected area.
2. Use your fingers or a soft-bristled brush to rub the solution into the fabric.
3. Let the solution sit for 15 minutes to allow it to penetrate the stain. Then wash as usual using the hottest water recommended on the care label.
4. To remove stubborn or old grass stains from clothes, you can soak them overnight in a mixture of cool water and oxygen bleach before washing.

## Life Skill #15: What to do with Slacks

Properly folding and hanging your pants keeps them organized and helps maintain their shape and prevent wrinkles. To fold and hang your pants effectively, follow these steps:

1. Take hold of the hem of both pants with your hands. Make sure the crease stays put. Pant legs straddle the hanger.

2. To hang, pass one leg through the other and let the hem dangle about an inch above the crotch. Use one hand to firmly pinch the fold shut.

3. Flip the other pant leg over the first and thread it through the hanger backwards with your free hand.

4. Make sure the creases on the pants are straight. The hanger will no longer cause your pants to unhinge.

## Life Skill #16: When Buttons Fall Off

Sewing isn't just for girls. Everyone can benefit from learning how to sew. It saves money, allows for unique gifts, and enhances home decor.

1. Put 24 inches of thread into your needle and draw it halfway through.

2. Knot the ends together once they are the same length on both sides of the needle.

3. From the wrong side of the fabric, poke the needle through and nearly yank the thread through.

4. The buttonhole is created by passing the needle and thread back and forth between the front and rear of the button.

5. Thanks to your repeated efforts, the button side of the cloth will now have an X shape.

6. After positioning the button at the X, pass the needle through one of the buttonholes, beginning on the wrong side of the fabric.

7. Cover the button with a spare needle or toothpick, and thread the needle back through the opposite hole. Tighten the thread.

8. With a tight, even tension on the thread, feed it through the button holes a total of three times, passing through opposite holes each time.

9. Wrap the thread around its base to prevent the button from coming loose. To do this, you should make six close loops around the bottom.

10. With the cloth pulled tautly, insert the needle to the wrong side of the fabric at the button's base and finish the thread with an overhand knot.

## Life Skill #17: Laundry Basics

Doing laundry might not be the most exciting task, but it's an essential life skill. But don't worry. Washing your clothes is way easier than it seems. Follow these ten easy steps for washing and drying clothes:

1. Sort laundry into lights and darks to prevent color bleeding.
2. Always read and follow care labels when washing clothes. Some items may be labeled "dry clean only" and should not be washed with water.
3. Check for stains and spills before washing. Use stain remover or detergent paste to ensure clean clothes.
4. Add the detergent.
5. Adjust water temperature based on clothing color. Hot/warm for whites/light colors, cold for darker clothes to prevent fading.
6. Place your clothes inside to load the washing machine, ensuring not to overload so it has space for the clothes to move freely during the wash cycle.
7. Close washer, select cycle, set timer for 45 min check.
8. When the washer is done, transfer the load to the dryer.
9. Maintaining a clean dryer vent is important for fire prevention and energy savings.
10. Add dryer sheets or balls for freshness and less static, set options/timer, and start the drying cycle.

**Dry Cleaning**

Dry cleaning uses special solvents to remove dirt, stain, and odors instead of water and detergent to clean delicate fabrics and clothes with intricate details. Remember these key details when it comes to dry cleaning:

1. Dry cleaning uses solvents.
2. Suitable for delicate fabrics like silk, wool, cashmere, velvet, and other sensitive materials.
3. Performed by professional cleaners who have the expertise and specialized equipment to handle different type for fabrics and stains.
4. Often pre-treat stains before the actual cleaning process.
5. Always check care labels and inspect each garment before and after cleaning process.
6. Minimizes clothes damage and helps extend the life of your clothes.
7. Convenience and save time.

## Life Skill #18: Dressing Right for the Occasion

Looking good isn't just about fashion. It's about knowing how to dress for different occasions. Here are some tips to help you boost your confidence and feel comfortable in social settings.

### Weddings

The wedding invitation, the time of day, and the season will all play a role in helping you decide what to wear. Wedding guests usually dress up to show respect for the couple getting married. Gentlemen, your attire should match the formality of the event. Dressing appropriately in a suit, sport coat, blazer, or evening suit is always appropriate. Check if a black tie is required.

## Business Dinner

A suit or blazer with a tie is always a safe bet. If the dress code is "business casual," a tie is not necessary.

## Graduation

Choose comfortable and appropriate attire for your graduation party. Stylish yet comfortable shoes are a good choice for moving around during the ceremony.

## Job Interview

Dress professionally for a job interview. Wear a business suit or business casual attire like khakis or dress pants with a button-down shirt, belt, and clean shoes. Ensure your outfit reflects the company culture and the position you are applying for.

## Religious Ceremony

Dress formally for the religious ceremony, preferably in a suit, jacket, or coat that reaches at least to your knees. Due to the importance of the occasion, more formal attire is required.

## Funeral

Although there is no legal requirement in the United States to wear black while mourning, it is important to dress appropriately and respectfully for the occasion. Sticking to dark colors and classic cuts is recommended to avoid offending to anyone during this solemn time.

**Dates and Other Social Events at School**

If you want to look your best and stand out for dates and school-related events, why not try something different than your usual jeans. A unique outfit can really make you feel confident and show off your personal style.

## Life Skill #19: How to Tie a Tie

If you're looking to dress up for a special event or a day at the office, knowing how to tie a tie is a must for any guy. Here are three tie knots that are commonly used and easy to learn:

**1. The Four-In-Hand Tie Knot**

1. The tie should be hung around your neck, with narrow end shorter than the wide end about 12 inches.

2. Wrap the wide end around the narrow one and tuck it back under.

3. Bring the wide end around the front of the narrow end twice more.

4. Thread the wide end through the loop's back opening.

5. Pull the wide end of the tie down through the front knot, holding the front with your index finger. Carefully tighten the knot by sliding it up and adjust to the desire position. A knot in the middle.

## 2. The Half-Windsor Tie Knot

1. The tie should be hung around your neck, with narrow end shorter than the wide end about 12 inches.

2. Wrap the wide end around the narrow one and tuck it back under the narrow one.

3. Insert the wide end through the space between your tie and collar.

4. Rotate the wide end clockwise, crossing the narrow part from right to left at the front.

5. Reverse the loop and feed the wide end back through it.

6. Pull wide end through the front knot and snug it up with both hands.

## 3. The Full Windsor Tie Knot

1. The tie should be hung around your neck, with narrow end shorter than the wide end about 12 inches. Loop

wide end through collar and bring forward by pulling it down.

2. Place the wider end on the right, behind the narrower one.

3. Feed the wide end through it. The future site of the tie knot should now look like a triangle.

4. Pull the wide end from right to left to round the triangle.

5. Insert the wide end inside the loop a further three times.

6. Feed the wide end through the front knot  and pull the ends of the knot together and make sure it's centered.

By mastering these skills, you can present yourself with pride, professionalism, and confidence.

# Chapter 3

## Home Management

As Mitchell grows up and starts taking care of his own place, he's discovering how important it is to handle things around the house. You know, like when you need your dad's help, but you also want to learn to do stuff yourself? In this chapter, you will learn how to use power tools, measure accurately, fix common issues, and master cleaning and painting, enabling you to take charge of your home and create a space you can be proud of. Discover vital skills for maintaining a neat and smoothly operating house.

## Life Skill #20: Know How to Use Power Tools

Learning how to use power tools may seem unnecessary, but it can be quite helpful in doing home repairs yourself. So, it's always a good idea to familiarize yourself with them.

**Safety First**

Always use caution when operating a power tool to avoid risks. Follow guidelines to minimize risks and stay safe.

- Adhere to any warnings and instructions provided by the maker.

- Protect your eyes, and don't wear loose clothing.

- Use leather gloves if at all possible.

- Verify that all necessary safety measures are in place and functioning.

- To avoid injury, never use broken equipment or instruments.

- Hold on tight to your tools at all times.

- Put on a dust mask before you start sanding.

- While using a noisy power tool, protect your ears with earplugs or earmuffs.

- Long hair should be restrained.

- Always use a GFCI (ground fault circuit interrupter) outlet while operating power equipment outside.

## Common Power Tools for Beginners

Start with small, simple power tools before moving on to larger, pricier ones. Here are some of the recommendation:

1. **Sander**: Sanding machines help to smooth surfaces quickly and efficiently. For best results, use a 1/4-sheet pad sander for a polished finish.

2. **Cordless Drill:** A power drill is not only useful for making holes in different sizes, but it is also versatile enough to be used with a range of attachments such as wire brush wheels, driver bits, sanding drums, and more.

3. **Jigsaw:** A jigsaw is a small saw with a thin blade that moves up and down, ideal for intricate or curved cuts.

4. **Circular Saw:** Circular saws are highly versatile power saws that can easily cut through various materials such as plywood, boards, and large pieces of trim with ease.

5. **Chainsaw:** Chainsaws are powered by electricity, compressed air, or gasoline and are used for cutting trees.

These handheld power tools are often affordable and accessible, with prices typically below sixty dollars. You can easily purchase them online or at hardware stores.

## Life Skill #21: Using a Tape Measure

Getting the hang of using a tape measure the right way and understanding its units of measurement is crucial for all kinds of tasks. You'll use it when you are sizing up spaces for furniture, checking out how big your garden is, or doing some cool DIY projects. Once you measure like a pro, you'll feel totally in control and ready to take on any project or task that comes your way.

## Read a Tape Measure

Reading a tape measure involves identifying the unit, whether imperial (inches) or metric( centimeters), and understanding the marking. The whole inches are represented by the longest lines in the imperial units, half inches by slightly shorter lines, and quarter inches by the shortest lines. In the metric system, longer lines represent whole centimeters, slightly shorter lines represent half centimeters, and the smallest lines represent millimeters. Always start measuring from zero, identify whole number first, and practice regularly to enhance accuracy. This practical skill is essential for DIY projects and carpentry, providing measurement capabilities for various tasks.

## Safety Tips

When retracting the blade and hook of a tape measure, it's essential not to let them snap back too quickly. This can cause serious injuries, as the hooks can flail violently. Even though it may seem convenient to have a fast retraction, it can be very dangerous. Additionally, some tape measures have steel blades with sharp edges, regardless of cost or quality. These edges may not seem very sharp initially, but they can become dangerous when moving quickly.

# Life Skill #22: Nailing Safety with a Hammer

A hammer is a like a trusty sidekick for all kinds of home jobs, from hanging up pictures to fixing up furniture or even building projects. But remember, safety always come first when using a hammer to prevent accidents or injuries. By following proper guidelines and precautions, you can safely wield a hammer and effectively complete your tasks.

## 1. Have a Plan

Developing a strategy is the first step to completing a task safely. Don't immediately start swinging wildly; rather, consider where you're swinging, what you hope to achieve, and how hard you need to swing your hammer before you do so. Injuries to yourself and others are possible if you use a hammer without a plan.

## 2. Inspect Your Hammer

The hammer's head must be securely fastened to the handle. The head may cause major injury or damage if it flies off the handle and hits someone or something. Do not use the hammer if it is really old and rusted.

### 3. Wear Safety Goggles

Hammering can cause debris to fly, or the hammer's claw might accidentally hit your eyes. Therefore, safety eyewear should be worn at all times and fastened securely.

### 4. Wear Gloves

Gloves are a necessity when handling anything that could hurt your hands. Grip-equipped gloves can help you keep control of your hammer and protect your hands from calluses and other minor wounds.

### 5. Look Before You Swing

Before bringing down the hammer, check your left and right flanks and rear. You won't endanger anyone (including yourself) by doing this. In addition, it prevents the hammer from snagging on nearby objects. Being aware of your surroundings is important, especially while working in a shared space.

### 6. Find a Good Grip

A rubberized grip is standard equipment on the lower part of the handle of most hammers. If that's not the case, then the bottom of the handle needs to be widened to improve grip. The force of your swing can be modulated by placing your thumb higher on the handle.

## 7. Maintain Accuracy

When using a hammer, it's possible to hit your fingertips accidentally. Make a few practice swings with the hammer, ensuring the target is in the middle of the head. Swing lightly at first, then harder as you drive the nail deeper into the wood. Take your hand away from the nail when it is firmly in place and will not budge. You could injure yourself if you use a hammer wrongly. Swinging with your entire arm will prevent you from overusing your shoulder or wrist.

## 8. Always Keep a First Aid Kit Handy

Accidents can happen despite precautions. Be prepared by having a well-stocked first aid kit readily available for any minor injuries.

# Life Skill #23: Using a Hand Saw

Just like a hammer, you will need a handsaw for many things. For example, you need it to cut and shape various wooden objects. But unfortunately, many people do not know how to use a handsaw properly. Let's discuss it.

**Use a Hand Saw**

**Step 1: Clamp Material**

Whether manual or powered, saws require careful setup to ensure clean cuts and minimal damage. Clamp the material to the table or bench before you try to saw it. This will help you maintain a straight line of cut and keep your material in place. Using safety eyewear while cutting wood is recommended.

### Step 2: Mark Cut

Mark the location of your cut using a pencil and a carpenter's square, ruler, or measuring tape. For a clean, precise slice, this is a must.

### Step 3: Start Cut

Carefully drag the saw along the marked line to cut a notch. Maintain a consistent downward force on the material you're sawing while slowly feeding the saw's teeth into the wood. You'll make your first incision here.

### Step 4: Cut Deeper

Keeping the saw at an incline, gently push down to begin sawing. Verify the straightness of your blade and mark by looking down the length of your saw to avoid binding. Binding occurs when you saw too aggressively or quickly, have a dull or bent blade, or work with damp wood. Avoiding binding requires a blade that is both straight and sharp and some additional lubricant. Do not use the saw with your hands on the offcut (the section of the board you cut off the longer length). Never pick up the snipped-off fragment.

### Step 5: Saw Through

After preparing a shallow groove, proceed to saw slowly and deliberately through the wood. Keep the knife's edge perpendicular to your intended cut. You may correct a crooked cut by angling the saw.

### Step 6: Finish Cut

Keep going until the wood is completely gone. During the final pass, go easy on the pressure to prevent splintering. If you want a nice finish on your material, you can sand the edges with a fine-grit sandpaper.

# Life Skill #24: Unclog All the Things

We've all been there! Dealing with clogged drains can be a real hassle. But guess what? You don't have to wait for a plumber to save the day. Learning how to unclog drains yourself is not only a valuable skill but also saves you time and money. Here are simple methods and handy tools to help you out.

1. **Remove the clog by hand.** If the clog is visible and near the surface. Put on some rubber gloves and try to remove the blockage. A wire coat hanger will do the

trick if you need something with a little more length or leverage.

2. **Use a drain snake.** A drain snake is a metal-wired gadget that can break up or pull away obstacles. To navigate the pipe, insert the snake into the drain and turn the hand crank. For clogged toilets, disposable plastic versions are also available.

3. **Use a plunger**. Plungers are not only helpful in the bathroom; they can also be used to unclog kitchen sinks. Choose a plunger with a cup shape that fits snugly over the drain opening. To generate suction, make a tight seal and perform regular up-and-down thrusts. If necessary, repeat.

4. **Use a pot of boiling water.** When a drain snake has failed to clear a drain of soap scum or cooking grease, and there are no obvious obstacles in the pipe, hot water might break up the softer buildup. If necessary, repeat.

5. **Use a natural drain cleaner**. Depending on the clog's severity, a mixture of white vinegar and baking soda may be equally helpful. One cup of baking soda and one cup of vinegar should be poured down the drain. Wrap a towel or drain stopper around the drain and leave the mixture in there for at least an hour to do

its job. Use scalding water to rinse. If necessary, this process should be repeated.

6. **Remove and clean the drain trap**. It's not uncommon for a clog to be lodged in the U-shaped pipe beneath the sink's garbage disposal. To collect the water that flows from the u-pipe, clear the area. Loosen the nuts on both ends of the pipe using a plumber's wrench while holding the pipe steady with your other hand. Remove any obstructions by flushing the pipe into the bucket. Remove the u-pipe, clean it, and then replace it.

## Life Skill #25: Safely Turning Off the Power

Knowing how to turn off the main circuit breaker is crucial for your safety during emergencies, like fires or fixing electrical problems around the house. With this skill in your toolkit, you can keep things safe and sound.

**Turning Off the Main Breaker**

1. **Open the panel door.** Find the main breaker panel and make sure the area around is dry. Lift the cover to uncover the panel's metal door. The following actions will turn out all of the lights in the house, so be sure

you have a flashlight handy if your main breaker panel is in a basement or other dark interior space.

2. **Identify the main circuit breaker.** Look at the circuit breakers in the panel to locate the main breaker, which is often situated between two vertical columns of branch circuit breakers.

3. **Shut off the main circuit breaker.** Put the main breaker's lever in the "OFF" position cautiously. All of the lights and appliances in the house should go out at the same moment as the electricity is cut off at the branch circuit breakers.

4. **Test for power.** Check numerous outlets around the house using a non-contact circuit tester to ensure the power is off. Homeowners frequently confused the main circuit breaker with the secondary one; therefore, it is essential to check for power to be sure.

**Restoring the Power**

When you're done making repairs to the circuit, just move the lever on the main breaker to the "ON" position to restore electricity. Because doing so can cause a significant power surge to be sent to all the circuits at once, experienced electricians typically perform this by first turning off all branch circuit breakers, then turning on the main circuit breaker, and finally turning on each individual circuit. Some breakers have a toggle that must be pushed all the way past the "OFF" position before the breaker can be turned back "ON"; this allows the spring mechanism to reset the breaker.

## Life Skill #26: When You Need to Turn off the Water

It's essential to know how to turn off the water in your house in case of emergencies or plumbing issues.

**Turning Off the Main Valve**

Water shutoffs should be done only in emergencies or when doing plumbing repairs, although occasionally closing and reopening the valves might be helpful. This will prevent them from freezing in place, allowing you to quickly turn off the water supply in the event of an actual emergency.

**Find the Main Shutoff Valve.**

Depending on your geographic location and the age of your home, the main shutoff valve may be located in a different room. There are two valve handles: gate valves (which resemble a spigot) and ball valves (which look like a lever). The main water shutoff valve is typically situated outside in warmer climates. The most likely locations are on an exterior wall or in a readily accessible underground box. Typically, this will be a cement box set into the ground next to your curb.

Putting a long screwdriver into the "lock," turning it counterclockwise, and then tilting the screwdriver toward the box's edge may be all that's needed to open the lid. If a screwdriver is ineffective, you can find a "meter key" at any hardware store.

- It is against the law to mess with the water meter or the side that shuts off the water from the city.

It's typically located on an inside wall in the basement, close to the front of the home, in colder climates. The valve could be in the garage if your house were built over an underground parking area.

- Do not adjust the pressure regulator, which is placed above the valve.

**Turning Off the Water Supply**

If the lever on your ball valve is perpendicular to the water pipe, then water is supplied to your home. The angle must be exactly 90 degrees for it to be correct. If your gate valve is shaped like a circular spigot, you must crank it clockwise until it stops providing water.

## Life Skill #27: Hanging Pictures

Making your space truly yours is all about the details, and hanging picture is one way to add personality and charm to your living area. Your artwork and photos will be exhibited and appreciated differently if you know how to do it right.

## How to Hang Pictures

Although it's generally accepted that artwork should be displayed at eye level, there are valid arguments for displaying some pieces higher or lower.

### 1. Measuring

- 57 to 60 inches from the ground is ideal for hanging a painting or picture so that most people can see it.
- Follow this equation: Frame height divided by 2, minus the height of the frame minus the height of the hanging hardware, plus 57, 58, 59, or 60.
- The final tally is the height (inches from the floor) plus the wall anchor placement.

### 2. Hanging

Use the most secure hanging technique for hanging paintings. To prevent frames from tipping or swaying, use two picture hangers.

1. Screw in a pair of D-rings on the frame's rear, one on each end.

2. Mark the wall with a pencil for each hook once you've selected where to hang the artwork, then use a level to ensure they're all the same height.

3. Hammer a picture hook into each of the wall marks.

4. Lift it up and place the D-rings on the picture hooks.

## Life Skill #28: Fixing Holes in Walls

Taking care of your living space is not just about responsibility, it's about making your place truly awesome. One of the handy skills you have to have in your toolkit is fixing those wall holes. It will save you some serious cash that you can use for things you really love.

**Patching a Small Hole**

Repairing a hole in the drywall with lightweight spackle is possible if the hole is smaller than a quarter.

**Step 1: Fill the hole**

Fill the crack with a spackle and smooth it with a putty knife. Fill the hole and "feather" the edges.

**Step 2: Wait for it to dry**

The directions or box for your spackling product should tell you how long you have to wait before touching the area again.

Some spackle has an initial dark hue but dries to a white finish.

### Step 3: Sand the area

Sand the entire surface down to a smooth finish using fine-grit sandpaper.

### Step 4: Repeat if necessary

### Patching a Larger Hole

The following approach can patch a hole larger than a quarter but smaller than around 8 inches across.

### Step 1: Prepare the area

The margins of drywall holes are rarely perfectly round, so you'll need a utility knife to clean them up.

### Step 2: Apply the patch

Use a piece of drywall cut to the appropriate size to cover the damage. To do this, peel off the patch's adhesive backing and adhere it directly over the damaged area, positioning the hole in the patch's center. Apply consistent pressure around the hole to help the patch adhere to the wall.

### Step 3: Apply mud

Use the putty knife to spread the joint compound (mud/spackle) over the patch. Fill the hole with mud using the feathering method, working outward toward the solid wall. The patch acts as a filter, allowing only a fraction of the spackle to pass through. This is preferable because it allows you to repair inner drywall damage by increasing the wall thickness on the exterior.

## Step 4: Wait

Follow the instructions on the packaging for drying the joint compound. A timeframe of up to 24 hours is possible.

## Step 5: Reapply

If the hole isn't completely filled in or the wall is still shaky, apply another coat of mud and let it dry for the specified period of time.

## Step 6: Sand

Use fine-grit sandpaper to smooth the wall after the mud has dried. If required, prep the wall and paint it to match.

# Life Skill #29: Room-by-Room Cleaning

Cleaning isn't the most exciting thing, but it's a great skill when you eventually have your own place. It will keep things manageable and critical for your health and mood.

## Steps for General Cleaning

### 1. Declutter Before Deep Cleaning

Everything that does not belong in the space should be discarded or relocated to a more appropriate location.

## 2. Start High, Go Low

The ceiling, ceiling light fixtures with bulbs, ceiling trim, walls, the remaining trim, and baseboards are the order in which you should clean the room's huge, difficult-to-reach surfaces.

## 3. Deep Clean Windows

Cleaning windows is an easy task with a substantial payoff. Cleaning the tracks and sills first is a must. The window should next be sprayed from top to bottom with glass cleaner.

## 4. Remove Dust from Surfaces

Apply furniture cleaning and polish to a soft cloth and wipe down all remaining hard surfaces, including shelves, wood furniture, built-ins, etc.

## 5. Deep Clean the Floors

Use furniture sliders to make moving heavy items much simpler. Clean hard floors with a microfiber mop and a cleaner, then vacuum the cracks and crevices. Those who have carpets should clean them.

## Cleaning Specific Rooms

## 1. Bedroom

- Launder Bedding
- Freshen Mattress
- Declutter Closet

## 2. Kitchen

- Polish Cabinets
- Deep Clean in and Around Appliances
- Tidy Countertops
- Bonus Deep Cleaning Task

## 3. Bathroom

- Wash Shower Curtain
- Make Shower Doors Sparkle
- Declutter Vanity and Cabinets

## 4. Living Room and Family Room

- Freshen Furniture
- Dust Frames
- Dust Under Electronics

# Life Skill #30: Paint Like a Pro

Ready to transform your space ? Painting a room is an easy and satisfying job to give your place a new look. These tips will help you quickly revamp your area and make you look like a pro.

**Painting a Room**

## 1. Clean and Prep the Walls

Dust, filth, and grease spots can blemish an otherwise flawless sheen, but they're easy to get rid of with water, a drop or two of mild dish washing soap, and a cellulose sponge.

## 2. Tape the Trim, Window, and Door frames

The painter's blue tape can be applied a week in advance, so remember to use it. Before the paint dries on the wall, remove the tape so it doesn't pull off with the paint

## 3. Prime the Walls

The finish coat will look more professional and uniform after being painted over with a new coat of primer.

## 4. Brush Hard-to-Reach Spots Before You Roll

Use a two-inch angled brush to apply paint around the trim and in wall corners where a roller won't go. Leave a space of two to three inches around windows, doors, and trim.

### 5. Use the W Method with the Roller

Start at a wall's corner and roll in a W pattern that covers three square feet; fill in the space without raising the roller for maximum efficiency. Keep going until you've completed the whole thing. Using this method, roller markings are less likely to be noticeable. Painting one wall at a time ensures a smooth finish.

### 6. Paint the Trim Last

Use a small brush to paint the trim around edges for precision and a neat look.

### 7. Wait

Allow the trim to dry, removing tape, and enjoy the fresh look!

# Chapter 4

## Know Your Way Around a Kitchen

When Jason started living on his own, he could only make grilled cheese sandwiches and ramen noodles. Although they helped him get through his freshman year of college, he soon realized that his diet was not particularly nutritious and that he wanted to broaden his culinary horizons to better his general health. In this chapter, we will explore a range of basic cooking techniques to improve your culinary skills.

## Life Skill #31: How to Set a Table

You could ask, "Why take the time to learn the proper method for setting the table? That won't make a difference in how the food tastes." Setting the table may seem small, but it says much about how you caring about your guests and making your meals feel delectable! Imagine impressing your friends or family with a perfectly set table. It's like leveling up your meal game. So, let's learn the art of setting the table together. You will be the host with the most in no time!

## Beautifully Basic

Napkins, forks, knives, and spoons are the minimum for a proper table setup. Fold the napkin in half and set it on the table, two inches to the left of the dish, where you can rest your fork. The knife should be placed to the right of the plate with the blade pointing toward the plate. A finger's width to the right of the knife, place the spoon. A glass of water over the knife is the finishing touch to a well-laid table. Although simple, your guests will love the familiar feel!

## Casual and Complete

Pick up where we left off with the basic table setting, but don't be afraid to dress it up with some finer cutlery and napkins. Set your napkin next to your plate with a goofy knot on it for a fun touch. If a dinner party occurs, set the table with a salad and soup bowl. To the right of the water glass, picture a wine glass.

## A Formal Finish

Ensure that your guests have everything they require for an unforgettable formal dinner. Put a salad fork beside the ordinary fork. Stack a soup spoon alongside the spoon. Stack the dishes using a dessert spoon. Because there are more courses, more silverware is often used in more formal settings. Place a bread plate and knife above each guest's napkin if you're serving bread. If you intend to serve a variety of wines, make sure you have enough wine glasses available.

## Life Skill #32: How to Sharpen Knives

Have you ever had a frustrating time in the kitchen with a dull knife while cooking? Not only it's risky, but it also makes preparation more difficult and reduces the appeal of the final product. A dull knife needs more force to cut, and it's easy for the blade to slip off the tough onion peel and cut your finger. Learning how to sharpen a kitchen knife with a whetstone or sharpener will help you avoid cutting yourself while cooking and preserve the quality of your meal.

### Sharpen with a Whetstone

Whetstones are great tools for sharpening blades since they function similarly to sandpaper in giving your knives a cutting edge. To ensure efficient sharpening, the whetstone must be fully wet in water for 5 to 10 minutes before usage. Holding your knife at a 20-degree angle, lightly rub the whetstone a few times on each side. For severely dull blades, begin with the coarse side and end with the fine side for a polished appearance. You can cook more safely and enjoyably by keeping your knives in good shape.

## Sharpen with a Knife Sharpener

If your knife is dull, press the blade into the coarse side, bring it toward you a few times, and then repeat with the fine side. Knowing how to utilize a knife sharpener in an emergency could be helpful. Remember that this sharpening equipment might not be excellent for your knife, so use a whetstone for your expensive Japanese chef's knife and this method for sharpening less expensive knives.

# Life Skill #33: Making Coffee When You Want It

Brewing your coffee isn't just about saving cash. It's about having your ideal cup of coffee whenever you crave it. It's a skill that can kickstart your day to impress your friends when they come over. Here's what you need for that ideal cup of coffee:

1. **Filtered water:** Make sure the water is pure and contaminant free so that the coffee's natural flavor can come through more.

2. **Correct proportions**: No matter what kind of machine you have, start with two tablespoons of ground coffee for every eight ounces of water.

3. **The right grind:** Depending on your coffee maker, the grind should be medium to medium-fine because coarser grounds would result in a weaker brew.

The following are the steps for making coffee. If you're using an automatic machine, just follow the manufacturer's guidelines:

1. **Place a filter into the coffee maker's basket.** The coffee beans should be ground to a medium or medium-fine consistency. Get some water to boil, then set it aside to cool down. Wet the filter by pouring water over it and letting it drain into your cup or coffee maker.

2. **Let the water out**. The coffee can be poured directly into the filter. Wet the ground beans with some water, then pour the rest of the water into the cup or coffee pot. Simple as pie!

## Life Skill #34: Cooking Eggs in Four Delicious Ways

Cooking eggs is healthful and one of the simplest and quickest ways to produce a great dinner. With only a few basic techniques, you can make scrambled, fried, hard-boiled, or poached eggs in no time. So, whether you're an experienced cook or just starting in the kitchen, eggs are a great go-to option for a delicious and stress-free supper. Here are four ways to prepare eggs at home:

## Scrambled

Making scrambled eggs is as simple as cracking eggs into a small bowl and whisking in milk, salt, and pepper. Add the egg mixture to the melted butter in the pan. Cook over low heat.

## Fried

Butter should be melted over low heat in a skillet. Crack an egg into a hot pan and season it with salt and pepper. You can flip the egg and cook it for a while longer to achieve the desired texture.

## Hard-Boiled

Put eggs in a pan and fill it with cold water until the eggs are submerged. Put the lid on the pan and place over high heat. When the water in the pan comes to a boil, remove it from the heat. Cover the eggs and let them sit for 15 minutes. After 15 minutes, transfer the eggs to a bowl of icy water for easy peeling, or keep them in the fridge for up to a week.

## Poached

Fill a minimum of 4 inches of water in a big pan and bring it to a low boil. Add a spoonful of white vinegar and mix well. Carefully crack an egg into a shallow bowl to avoid breaking the yolk. Using a wooden spoon, create a whirlpool in the water. The egg may be tossed into the churning liquid. Poached eggs can be perfectly cooked by flipping them over at regular intervals. For removing poached eggs from the water, a slotted spoon is perfect.

# Life Skill #35: Grilling the Perfect Steak

Steak is a summertime BBQ favorite for a good reason. However, grilling a steak can be difficult, especially since there appears to be no consensus on the perfect doneness (medium rare!). But it's easier and faster than you think. With these essential steak grilling tips, you'll be a master in no time.

## Steak Grilling Tips

1. **Clean and Season Your Grill:** After thoroughly cleaning, massage the grill with a naturally refined high-heat oil, such as avocado oil. Flare-ups can be avoided by putting the proper amount of oil in the pan. Brush the grates before and after each use to keep them clean and ready.

**2. Be Patient with Charcoal:** If you're attempting to use charcoal, be patient. If you let the coals burn evenly, a charcoal barbecue's rich, smoky flavor is worth the wait.

**3. Temper the Meat:** Meat needs to be tempered before it can be grilled properly. To prevent food poisoning, the steak must sit at room temperature for at least an hour before being grilled. You shouldn't wait more than 90 minutes, though.

**4. Don't Skimp on Seasoning:** Steak is best when seasoned with freshly cracked black pepper, kosher salt. Proper seasoning brings out the meat's natural flavors, making it flavorful.

**5. Leave the Steak Alone:** Leave the steak alone once you've thrown it on the grill. If you poke it, the meat may dry up, and if you move it around too much, the grill marks won't stick.

**6. Let it Rest:** Rest the steak for half the time it took to cook after removing it from the grill. Tenderness is improved when juices are redistributed throughout this phase.

# Life Skill #36: How to Cook Ribs

Grilled ribs are a mainstay of American barbecue, and with good reason: when done right, they're so soft that the meat practically falls off the bone, and they have a rich, savory flavor. Even though there are dedicated pit masters everywhere working to perfect their rib-grilling method, you don't have to wait for them to do it for you. Read on to find out the different types of ribs and how to easily cook pork and beef ribs at home.

## Grill Pork Spare Ribs, Pork Baby Back Ribs, and Beef Back Ribs

These ribs look and taste much like traditional ribs; therefore, they should be grilled low and slow.

1. If your butcher didn't do it for you, peel back the membrane from the ribs' underside the night before grilling. Simply slip a knife under the membrane and into the meat to loosen it, then peel it off with your fingertips.
2. It's best to marinate the ribs overnight.
3. Prepare your grill by cleaning it, preheating it on low, creating a heated basin, and lubricating the grates.
4. After marinating, remove the ribs and place them bone-side down on the grill over indirect heat.

5. Keep the meat covered and cook until it reaches an internal temperature of 180 to 195 degrees, turning it once or twice. This could take anywhere from one to two hours, depending on the size of your ribs.
6. Separate and eat after resting for at least 10 minutes.

**Grill Beef Short Ribs**

When grilled, short ribs benefit from being cooked at a lower temperature (about 145 degrees) and for a longer period of time than most other cuts. Just a little bit of salt and pepper brings out the full flavor of this cut.

1. Prepare your grill by cleaning it and heating it on high. Lubricate the slats.
   Put the short ribs on the grill after seasoning them with salt and pepper.
2. Turning the meat over often, cook it to an internal temperature of 145 degrees. Depending on the size of the ribs, this should take about 10 minutes.
3. Rest for 10 minutes, then serve.

## Life Skill #37: How to Grill Veggies

Cooking veggies on a grill brings out their entire flavor with minimal work and a certain level of excitement. Grilling vegetables improves their taste, so here are some basic methods for grilling vegetables that will bring out their natural sweetness and make them ideal to savor during the summer.

## Directly on the Grill

1. Grill to medium-high heat, or between 375 and 400F (on a gas grill).
2. Prepare your vegetables by marinating them or seasoning them with olive oil, salt, and pepper.
3. Vegetables that take the longest to cook should go at the back of the grill, where the heat is strongest, while those that cook the quickest should go toward the front.
4. Cook the vegetables for around 5 minutes with the lid closed.
5. After 5 minutes, remove the vegetables from the grill, starting with the ones closest to you that need the least cooking time.
6. Then, put the top back on and cook for a few more minutes or until they reach the desired doneness.

## Foil Pack Vegetables

1. Preheat the grill between 375 and 400 F (on a gas grill).

2. Prepare your vegetables by marinating or seasoning them with olive oil, salt, and pepper, then layering them between two sheets of heavy-duty aluminum foil.

3. Folding the foil in on itself creates a seal that prevents leakage.

4. Make a hole in the top of the foil with a fork or knife to release some of the steam.

5. Set the foil pack over the grill' open flame and cook for 20 to 25 minutes, turning once.

## Life Skill #38: Roasting and Carving the Perfect Turkey

Roasting a turkey for Thanksgiving might seem like a daunting task, but fear not! With some prep and a few simple steps, you can master the art of roasting and carving a delicious turkey for your feast. Here's a step-by-step guide to get you started:

**1. Thawing the Turkey:** The first step is to defrost the turkey. Allow 24 hours for every 4 pounds of frozen turkey to thaw. Plan ahead to ensure the turkey has completely thawed before cooking.

**2. Preparing the Turkey:** Remove the turkey from its packaging once it has thawed. Remove the neck and giblets and set them away for later use in creating gravy. Pat the turkey dry with paper towels to achieve crispy skin while roasting. Allow the turkey to come to room temperature for 8-12 hours. This step ensures that the turkey cooks evenly and that it is tender.

**3. Seasoning and Stuffing:** Sprinkle some salt and pepper within the turkey's cavity. Put the apple, herb sprigs, onion quarters, and lemon quarters inside.
To prepare a turkey for cooking, tuck its wings beneath its body and place it on a roasting rack in a roasting pan. Turkeys can sit more upright and comfortably by folding their wings under their bodies.

**4.Adding Flavor**: Using your fingertips, loosen and lift the skin slightly above the turkey's breasts. Next, put a few tablespoons of herb butter under the skin after you have completed the previous step. The turkey legs can be held together with simple twine. Spread the remaining herb butter all over the turkey's exterior.

**5. Preparing for Roasting:** Preheat the oven to 325°F (165°C). Place the turkey in a roasting pan, breast side up, and tuck the wings beneath the body for even cooking.

**5. Roasting the Turkey:** In a preheated oven, cook the turkey until the thickest part of the thigh reaches an internal temperature of 165°F (74°C). Halfway through the cooking time, check on the turkey. Check the turkey skin with an oven light to see if it's brown, and then tent the breast with foil to keep it from overcooking.

**Prepare the Turkey for Carving: A Step-by-Step Tutorial**

1. Rest the turkey for at least half an hour. The meat will absorb more flavor after some downtime.
2. Prepare a carving area.
3. Split the upper leg from the thigh on one side.
4. Cut the thigh bone away from the drumstick.
5. The breast and wing on the same side should be cut off.
6. Switch sides and do it again.
7. Separate the breasts and thighs.

## Life Skill #39: All the Ways to Cook Fish

Cooking fish can be done in various ways. However, it is easy to mess up if you are not careful. But with the right way, you can make some seriously delicious meals. When the fish is done, it changes color and flakes apart. That is your signal. A decent rule of thumb when cooking fish is 10 minutes for 2.5 inches of thickness. Grill your salmon for 5 minutes, flip it over, and cook it for an additional 5 minutes if the thickness portion of it is 2.5 inches. The cooking time should be adjusted based on the thickness of the fish. Here are some easy ways.

**Bake**

1. Preheat the oven to 450F.
2. Nonstick cooking spray should be used on a baking sheet or a shallow dish.
3. Season the fish to your liking and spread it in a single layer on a baking sheet.
4. Fish should be baked in a covered baking dish for 10 minutes for every inch of thickness.

**Sauté or Pan Fry**

This cooking method creates soft, crisp bites of food. Fish filets, shrimp, bay scallops, and slipper tails are some examples of seafood that work very well with this method. Strips of firm fish like cod or halibut can also be stir-fried.

1. Over medium heat, melt 1/4 inch of butter or oil in a nonstick frying pan.
2. Milk or beaten eggs might coat the fish before it is breaded.

3. Fish should be cooked for 4-5 minutes per side (per inch of thickness).

**Poach**

Wine, water, fish stock, or milk can be gently heated and used to prepare almost any fish.

1. The fish should be completely submerged in the liquid.
2. Filets should be cooked slightly below boiling, with the pan well covered.
3. Filets need only ten minutes of cooking time, but whole fish needs fifteen to twenty.
4. You can make a sauce out of the poaching liquid.

## Life Skill #40: How to Cook Pork Chops

Cooking pork chops is a fantastic skill, especially if you want to impress your friends and family with delicious meal. Pork chops are a tried-and-true crowd-pleaser that even the pickiest eaters will love. They are tender juicy and pair perfectly with sides like salad, potato bake, vegetables, and creamy garlic sauce. Searing pork chops in a very hot skillet for about 3 minutes, flipping them over, and finishing them in the oven is all it takes to make perfectly cooked pork chops every time. This method of preparation guarantees that they will be thoroughly cooked without drying out.

1. Chops should not be cooked straight from the refrigerator. Take the chops out of the fridge 30 minutes before you want to start cooking.

2. Salt the chops for half an hour before they go in the oven. This will give the salt an opportunity to enhance the meat's flavor and tenderness.

3. Season the chops with salt and pepper and dust them lightly with flour. This is the perfect time to break out your go-to spice rub.

4. After browning one side of the chops in a hot skillet, flip them over, reduce the heat to low, and cover the pan.

5. Since you covered the skillet, the heat will slowly brown the other side while gently cooking the meat in the middle. The chops will be juicy and soft after being cooked in this manner!

6. Put them on a clean platter immediately after cooking and tent with foil. At that time, the juices will have spread throughout the chops.

# Chapter 5

## Car Matters

Marcus's vehicle was behaving strangely, but it was still moving, so he proceeded with his journey. Imagine the shock on his face as he pulled up to a red light and noticed that the officer in the car next to him was waving at him to put his window down. The police called over, "You have a flat tire, son!" as he approached. Marcus had no idea this unexpected tire issue would become a watershed moment in his car-owning journey. The incident inspired him to take responsibility for his car's maintenance and gain the skills required to deal with various car-related issues. In this chapter, we'll go over the essential driving abilities that every driver should have.

## Life Skill #41: Navigating the DMV

Everyone has a friend or family member who has told a frightening story about a DMV experience. Perhaps you last visited when you were a young driver with a parent or guardian and needed a driver's license or permit. A trip to the DMV to register a vehicle, title it, or get a driver's license can be a nightmare. Here's a step-by-step guide to surviving a trip to the DMV.

Remember to bring the following paperwork the next time you visit the DMV:

**Proof of age and identity**

- Passports.

- Driver's licenses.

- State ID cards.

- Passport cards and/or enhanced driver's licenses.

- Voter registration cards.

- Social Security cards.


**Other things to bring and keep in mind:**

- Book an appointment.

- Make sure you have the right documentation.

- Pay attention to the holidays on the calendar.

- Early visits always make a difference.

- Proof of liability insurance.

- Get the cheapest auto insurance policy possible.

- Complete your procedure online.

- Eat and drink something before going to the Department of Motor Vehicles.

## Life Skill #42: Checking and Changing Oil

Almost any driver can quickly and easily check their car's or truck's engine oil. You might not want to change your engine oil, but you should be able to inspect it. Most automobiles require oil changes every three months or 3,000 miles. On the other hand, modern cars can travel farther due to engine advances and improved oil quality. Manufacturers recommend oil changes every 5,000 to 7,500 miles for newer vehicles as of September 2021, with specific models going up to 10,000 to 15,000 miles between changes. But you don't have to wait until the next oil change to see how your engine oil is holding up. You can monitor your engine oil for indicators of low levels or pollution between oil changes. So, let's check your engine oil by following these step by step:

1. Shutting off the engine is the first step in checking the oil, so do that first.
2. Find a Lint-Free Rag or old T-shirt to clean the dipstick.
3. Locate the dipstick under the hood using your owner's manual as a guide.
4. Check the oil while the car is still warm. Oil changes are best done after short drives.

5.  Lift the hood using the inside handle and prop it open safely.

6.  Locate the dipstick, which has a bright yellow or orange circle for the handle and is typically found on the left side of the engine.

7.  Pull the dipstick out, wipe it with your lint-free rag or old T-shirt and put it back.

8.  Pull the dipstick out again and check the tip of the dipstick for oil level, which is indicated by a "full" line or texture on the dipstick. There will be an amber hue to the oil.

9.  If the oil level is in the acceptable range, then you are good to go.

10. If the oil is low or dirty, it's time to change it.

## Life Skill #43: Changing a Flat Tire

Dealing with a flat tire becomes your top priority right away when you least expect it. Anyone can get a flat tire; and when it happens, you can handle it confidently if you know what to do. Changing a tire is the same process for a car, truck, van, or SUV. So, if you ever find yourself in a flat tire while driving, it is best to reduce speed gradually, activate the hazard lights, and look for a safe area to pull over. If you can, park in an empty lot or someplace with little foot traffic and follow these steps to change it safely:

1. Set parking brake.
2. Put out warning devices.
3. Place wheel wedges.
4. Remove hubcap.
5. Loosen lug nuts.
6. Position the jack under your car.
7. Lift vehicle using jack.
8. Completely unscrew lug nuts .
9. Remove flat tire.
10. Mount spare tire.
11. Replace lug nuts.
12. Slightly lower vehicle.
13. Tighten lug nuts with the wrench.
14. Finish lowering vehicle.
15. Put the hubcap back on.
16. Check tire pressure.
17. Put everything back in your vehicle.
18. Get your flat tire fixed.

# Life Skill #44: Jump-Starting a Car

Knowing how to jump-start a car can be quite helpful when you have a dead battery. It happens to everyone at some point: we turn the key and hear the dreaded click. But do not worry! Learning how to jump-start a car is simpler than you might think, and it can be the difference between being stranded and quickly getting back on the road.

**Jump-Start a Car, Step by Step:**

Learning how to do it on your own is relatively easy. But first, certain conditions must be satisfied. To begin, you'll need a jumper cord of some kind. The second thing you'll need is a willing helper among your fellow drivers.

1. Park with the two cars facing each other. Put on the parking brake for security purposes. Lift the hoods and find the power packs. If you need access, take off the plastic cover. Locate the battery's positive (+) and negative (-) terminals. Remove any rust or corrosion that may have formed.

2. Connect the positive terminal of the dead battery with the end of the red (positive) jumper cable. Then, join the other end of the red cable to the active battery's positive terminal. Then, join the other end of the red cable to the active battery's positive terminal.

3. Next, join the black (negative) jumper cable's other end to the functional battery's negative terminal. The unpainted metal surface of the deceased car's engine block should receive the other end of the black cable, which should be attached there. This creates a grounding point.

4. To jump-start a car with a dead battery, start a vehicle with a good battery and let it idle for a few minutes. Then try to start the dead car. Once it's running, disconnect the jumper cables carefully in reverse order.

5. Keep the recently jump-started automobile running for a minimum of 15-20 minutes to allow the battery to recharge.

6. If your car fails to start despite jump-starting or if you face recurrent battery problems, it's advisable to seek the assistance of a mechanic to identify and rectify any underlying issues.

## Life Skill #45: Driving a Stick Shift

Nowadays, most drivers opt for the ease of an automatic transmission. However, let's remember that learning to drive a manual transmission can be a valuable skill. Why, you ask? Well, it opens up a world of possibilities. Being proficient in stick shift driving can offer several advantages, including renting cars in foreign countries, borrowing friends' cars during emergencies, and having greater maneuverability on the road. If you're wondering where to start this journey, read on to discover how to begin your project.

**Drive a Manual Transmission Car**

1. Get comfortable with the pedals' positions and gear changes by spending time behind the wheel. A manual car has three pedals: the clutch pedal is on the left, the accelerator is on the right, and the brake is in the middle.
2. Press the clutch and turn the key to start the engine.
3. Press the clutch pedal down to disengage the engine from the wheels while the engine is running.
4. Shift to neutral. Look for "N" on the gear shift diagram.
5. Release the handbrake if engaged to allow the car to move freely.
6. Keep your foot on the brake as you release the clutch. The biting point will be when you notice the car moving slightly forward.
7. Apply some pressure to the accelerator gradually while releasing the clutch pedal slowly. The car will begin to move forward as you do this smoothly.
8. Depress the clutch pedal to disengage it before shifting gears. Select the appropriate gear, then carefully let go of the clutch while giving little pressure to the accelerator.
9. Downshift to lower gears sequentially (5-4-3-2-1)when slowing down or coming to a stop. Every time you shift gears, remember to release the clutch.

10. To totally stop the car, depress the clutch and brake at the same time. Put the car in neutral after you've stopped.

11. When parking, apply the handbrake, set the gearshift to neutral, and turn off the engine.

# Life Skill #46: Dealing with a Traffic Stop

Getting pulled over by the police can feel overwhelming for anyone. However, it's crucial to approach the situation with confidence and composure, whether it's a routine check or a minor offense. Being prepared can help you handle the situation with ease. The following advice can assist you in interacting with police enforcement, keeping yourself safe, and perhaps avoiding a penalty or arrest.

**1. Find a Safe Spot**

Find a secure place to stop once you see the police car flashing its lights at you to stop. Look for well-lit areas or a broad road shoulder if it's evening.

**2. Stay Calm and Follow Instructions**

Turn off the engine, keep your hands on the steering wheel to show that you are not a threat, and wait for the officer.

Politely provide documents when asked while remaining cordial and helpful.

### 3. Know Your Rights

You can politely ask about the reason for the stop without arguing.

### 4. Comply and Listen Carefully

Follow instructions for stepping out if needed and pay attention to the officer's explanation and decisions.

### 5. Stay Patient

Avoid sudden movements and wait patiently for the signal to leave safely before getting back to the road.

### Never, Never, Never...

- Reach for anything or make sudden movements as the police officer approaches your car.
- Argue with officer.
- Be rude.
- Talk about your rights, address any concerns later.
- Exit the vehicle until instructed to do so.

# Life Skill #47: Handling a Car Accident

We all hope we never have to deal with it, but knowing how to handle a car accident is a vital life skill everyone should be able to perform. Nobody intends to be in a car accident, but being ready can make a big difference in how things turn out. If a car accident occurs, you can take action to safeguard your interests. Here are some essential steps to approach the situation calmly and responsibly.

## 1. Remain Calm and Look for Any Injuries

Ensure you and everyone else in the car are secure and unharmed. Keeping cool and acting normally in the face of an accident will help you maintain your composure.

## 2. Move the Impacted Car to Safety

If your car is still operational, you should move it as far away from traffic as possible while staying at the accident scene. Use warning lights or road flares to warn oncoming vehicles.

## 3. Call 911 to Get Help

Dial 911 to report the accident and wait for the authorities to arrive.

## 4. Cooperate with the Police

Show the police officer your identification, driver's license, and proof of insurance. Respond to their inquiries and get their contact details. The insurance company will want to see the police report, so make sure to get one.

## 5. Exchange Information and Take Pictures

As part of your car accident checklist, you should always take photos of the damage to your vehicle and any other vehicles involved, even if the police report provides a formal record of the crash. Take pictures from different vantage points to demonstrate the exact location of the collision. Your claims adjuster can use these photos to understand better what happened and who is at fault. Obtain the other driver's contact details, including their name, phone number, address, and insurance company.

## 6. Start the Claims Process

You must notify your car insurance company regardless of who was at fault. Never forget that you can file a claim with either your own insurance provider or the other driver's. An automobile accident report to the police is optional but often helpful when filing an insurance claim.

## Life Skill #48: All the Things You Should Have in Your Vehicle

Always keep essential items in your car for emergencies and smooth running. Check them before a long trip, especially in a remote area. Here are the must-haves:

1. Owner's Manual.
2. Car Repair Information.
3. License, Insurance, and Registration.
4. Tire Jack, Spare Tire, and Lug Wrench.
5. Jumper Cables.
6. Tire Pressure Gauge.
7. WD-40.
8. Duct Tape.
9. Cleaning Supplies.
10. First Aid Kit.
11. Tactical Flashlight.
12. Reflective Triangles and/or Flares.
13. Multi-Tool.
14. Car Hammer.
15. Windshield Wiper Fluid.
16. Ice-Scraper or Snow-brush.
17. Warm Gear.

## Life Skill #49: Maintenance Schedule

Getting a car is just the beginning. Once you've got it, you must maintain it regular to keep it running smoothly for years to come. Maintaining a vehicle's proper operation requires regular service. Manufacturers recommend getting your car serviced at regular intervals. Specific service and maintenance intervals should be determined in with the dealer, owner's manual, or authorized service professional. Here's a car maintenance schedule based on mileage intervals.

## Every 3,000 to 7,000 Miles

According to the manufacturer's suggested car maintenance schedule, the oil and oil filter should be changed anywhere from 3,000 to 7,000 miles. You should inspect the power steering fluid, coolant, windshield washer fluid and wipers, transmission fluid, tires, and exterior lights.

## Every 15,000 to 30,000 Miles

A new air filter should be installed after 15,000 miles. At 20,000-mile intervals, make sure to inspect the battery and coolant. Changing the gasoline filter is a standard recommendation at 25,000-mile intervals. You should change your air filter and power steering fluid every 30,000 miles. Verify that the brake pads, suspension, and air conditioning are all in good working order.

## Every 35,000 to 50,000 Miles

Every 35,000 miles, the battery needs to be checked and possibly replaced. Every 40,000 kilometers, you should have the spark plugs and wires replaced and the ignition and suspension inspected. Both 45,000 and 50,000 miles call for another round of these checks.

**Every 60,000 Miles**

Change the power steering fluid, brake fluid, timing belt, and radiator hoses. Check the air conditioning, the tires, and the suspension. Regular inspections of the engine, transmission, cooling system, brakes, and suspension systems are just as crucial as oil changes and air filters to keep an engine running smoothly. The owner's manual for the most of vehicles includes a maintenance schedule that considers mileage.

## Life Skill #50: Backing Up a Trailer

Although backing up a trailer may initially appear difficult, with some practice and helpful tips, you can master it and drive with assurance. Whether you're towing for a camping vacation or moving, these techniques will make the process simpler and have you backing up like an expert in no time.

**Tip 1: Hand Placement**

Put your hands on the wheel at six o'clock to make it easier to steer the trailer: Move your hand left to turn left and right to turn right.

## Tip 2: Hand Placement

Put your hands on the wheel at six o'clock to make it easier to steer the trailer -- move your hand left to turn left and right to turn right.

## Tip 3: Visualize Separately

Consider your vehicle and trailer as separate objects. Imagine your car pushing the trailer with its rear. Like guiding a wheelbarrow, turn the wheel to the right by moving handles to the left, and do the opposite to turn to left.

## Tip 4: Make Wide Turns

Make it a wide turn at first and move slowly. Making the turns feel wide will help you better control the trailer. Avoid making sharp turns or increasing your speed because the trailer to jackknife ( twist at a severe angle).

## Tip 5: Keep the Trailer From Jackknifing.

It's important to avoid jackknifing in order to protect the towing car and trailer. When backing up, take it slow and correct any sharp turns by either pulling forward or steering the tow vehicle in the direction that the trailer is traveling.

# Chapter 6

## Basic CPR and Healthcare Advice

A s a result of his mother's influence, Kelvin never missed a doctor's appointment. She accompanied him and spoke on his behalf the entire time. When he turned 19 and called his mother to ask if she would schedule a doctor's appointment, she told him to "do it yourself." Can you imagine the shock on his face? How?? It dawned on him. He realized it was time to learn the basics of CPR and other essential health care.

## Life Skill #51: Learn CPR

Knowing how to perform CPR is a crucial skill that can make a life-saving difference in critical moments. CPR, or cardiopulmonary resuscitation, is an emergency procedure for a person experiencing cardiac arrest. During cardiac arrest, the heart stops pumping or beats too weakly to deliver oxygenated blood to the brain and other essential organs.

In these situations, every second counts. Before professional medical help arrives, you can help and provide immediate assistance to maintain the oxygen flow to the brain and other essential organs by performing chest compressions and rescue breathing. This simple yet vital action can be the difference between life and death. Let's learn and understand how to perform CPR effectively so we can be prepared to make a difference when it matters most.

**CPR for Adults**

1. Stack one hand on top of the other on the sternum, the imaginary line that runs between your nipples and right in the middle of your chest. Keep your body weight centered between your hands.
2. To begin CPR, compress the chest by pressing down around 2 inches at a pace of twice per second to get a reaction.
3. Between compressions, you should lift the patient's body weight, not your hands.
4. If you're confident, deliver two rescue breaths after 30 compressions.
5. Repeat and continue performing chest compressions and rescue breathing in 30:2 intervals until medical assistance arrives or the person awakens.

## Children 1 to 8 Years Old

Performing cardiopulmonary resuscitation (CPR) on a child aged 1 to 8 is quite similar to doing so on an adult.

1. The child should have his or her chest patted. Put both hands on the kid's sternum, or just one if they're tiny.
2. Start to compress the chest at a rate of around twice per second and a depth of around 2 inches.
3. Offer two rescue breaths after 30 chest compressions.
4. Repeat and continue performing chest compressions and rescue breathing in 30:2 intervals until medical help arrives or the child awakens.

## Infants

1. To provoke a reaction, flick the sole of the foot. This is the modern equivalent of extending one's hand to shake the older person's hand.
2. Position the two middle fingers of one hand above the heart.
3. Compress the chest. Put around 1.5 inches of pressure on the chest with your fingertips. As you would with an adult, perform two compressions per second.
4. Take rescue breaths. As you would with an older person, deliver two rescue breaths between each round of 30 chest compressions if you are trained.

## Life Skill #52: How to Save Someone Who Is Choking

Choking is a life-threatening when an object or food blocks the airway, obstructing airflow.  It can affect people of all ages, but it's common with food in adults and small objects in preschoolers. Choking prevents oxygen from reaching the brain, making it critical to take immediate action when someone is choking.

Allow a person who is choking to continue coughing if they can do so forcefully. The object may be expelled with a cough. First aid should be administered to someone who is unable to cough, speak, cry, or laugh loudly. Here are some suggestions from the American Red Cross:

1. Give five back blows. If an adult is choking, stand to one side and slightly behind them. Support the person's weight by placing an arm across their chest. Turn the person's upper body so that their feet are on the floor. Use the heel of your hand to deliver five distinct blows to the space between the target's shoulder blades.
2. Give five abdominal thrusts. Five abdominal thrusts, popularly known as the Heimlich technique, should

be administered if back blows fail to dislodge the object.

3. Use a combination of five hits and five thrusts to break through the obstruction.

If you want to give someone abdominal thrusts, you should:

1. For stability, step forward with one foot. Encircle your own midsection with your arms. Lightly nudge the person forward.
2. Clench one of your hands into a fist. Position it so that it's slightly above the navel.
3. Use your free hand to grab the fist. Quickly thrust upward into the abdomen (belly button) as if you were trying to raise the individual off the ground. Avoid inflicting severe trauma on a person's internal organs by applying strong pressure with care.
4. Perform five thrusts to the stomach. Verify that the obstruction has been cleared. When necessary, repeat.

Don't attempt abdominal thrusts if the patient is pregnant or if you can't wrap your arms around their tummy.

To administer abdominal thrust to yourself:

1. Position your hands at the center of the bottom of your breastbone, below where your ribs join.
2. Quickly push your fist into their chest and press down hard. This is the same motion used in the Heimlich technique.
3. Do it again and again until you can breathe normally again.

## Life Skill #53: The Fireman Carry- a Lifesaver Skill

Have you ever wondered how firefighters, lifeguards, and soldiers remove people from dangerous situations? They've got special gear and training for sure. Some of that training includes using this Fireman's Carry technique. This stand-out technique can minimize the potential for injury while maintaining efficiency. Whether it's a fire or any other emergency, the Fireman's Carry is a skill you'll want to have for the safety and survival of all. Ready to learn it? It won't be so fluid the first few times you try it, but it will get easier!

Here's how it's done (as a right - side dominant person -- flip it for a dominant left):

1. First, help the injured person stand if they are able.

2. Mirroring them, use your L hand to grasp the victim's opposite arms, their R.

3. Step with your dominant R foot between their legs.

4. Then, in one sweeping motion, move the victim toward you and put your head under the R arm of the person as you swing them over.

5. In the same fluid motion, wrap your R arm around the back of his or her R knee.

6. Stoop down and put their weight over your shoulders.

7. Distribute the victim's weight evenly by using your L hand to put their R hand into your R hand. Completing this arm circle around your neck centers their weight over your center of gravity.

8. Use your legs to press up and stand with the additional weight.

9. Carefully move the victim towards somewhere safe.

## Life Skill #54: How to Care for Cuts and Scrapes

Cuts from knives and glass can happen during everyday activities like cooking and cleaning. They might seem intimidating at first, but most cases, you can manage them with some basic first aid at home. Check out these simple methods to take care of scrapes and cuts:

1. Wash your hand to avoid infection.
2. Elevate the injured area and apply mild pressure with a clean bandage or cloth to stop the bleeding.
3. Clean the wound. Wash the wound to remove the blood. Keep the wound moist with running water to reduce the risk of infection. Clean the area around the cut with soap. However, avoid rubbing soap into the wound.
4. If you see any debris or grim remains in the wound, remove it. Use alcohol-sanitized tweezers to remove any grime or debris. Avoid using harsh chemicals like hydrogen peroxide or iodine. You should see a doctor if you're having trouble clearing the area.
5. Apply a thin coating of petroleum jelly or an antibiotic ointment to keep the area moist and reduce the likelihood of scarring. Some people may develop a slight rash from using ointments because of the presence of certain components. Stop applying the cream if you develop a rash.
6. Cover the wound with a bandage, rolled gauze, or gauze secured with paper tape to protect it from dirt and prevent further injury. You can leave it open if it is just a scratch or scrape. Repeat at least once a day and more often if the bandage gets damp or soiled.
7. Get vaccinated against tetanus. If the wound is deep or unclean and you haven't received a tetanus vaccine in

the prior five years, you should get one.

Look out for any symptoms of infection. You should consult a doctor if there is redness, growing pain, drainage, warmth, or swelling around the wound.

## Life Skill #55: How to Treat Burns

First-degree burns are pretty common. They can happen when you touch something hot or spend too much time in the sun. Unlike those deeper second or third-degree burns, these only mess with the top layers of your skin. Redness, discomfort, and slight swelling are all symptoms of a first-degree burn. But you can handle them at home if you know what to do. Dermatologists recommend the following steps for how to treat burns:

**First-Degree Burns**

1. Cool the burn. Put the burned area under cold running water or use cold, moist compresses immediately. Keep doing this for at least 10 minutes or until the discomfort disappears.

2. Slather some petroleum jelly two or three times a day. Avoid putting anything on the burn that could harbor bacteria, such as ointments, toothpaste, or butter. Do not use antibiotic creams or ointments.

3.  Use a sterile, nonstick bandage to cover the burn. Keep the area covered and bandaged if blisters appear; this will let them heal on their own. Avoid picking at the blisters.

4.  Take into account getting some kind of over-the-counter pain reliever. Painkillers like acetaminophen and anti-inflammatory drugs like ibuprofen can do wonders.

5.  Shade the area so it doesn't get too hot. After the burn has healed, it is important to prevent further sun damage by staying in the shade, donning UV-protective clothing, or using sunscreen with an SPF of 30 or higher. This is especially helpful for people with darker skin tones, as the redness of a burn can linger for weeks.

**Severe Burns**

1.  Keep the burned victim safe from danger. As much as possible, keep the individual you're treating away from the cause of the burn.

2.  Before approaching someone, who has suffered an electrical burn, ensure the power has been turned off. Don't try to pull out a garment that got caught in a fire. Verify that the burned individual is still breathing. If

you know how to perform rescue breathing, start doing so.

3. Take off any tight clothing or jewelry, focusing on the burned region and the neck. Almost immediately, the affected areas will swell after a burn.

4. Dress the wound. Wrap some gauze or a clean rag loosely around the affected region.

5. Raise the burning area  above the heart level if possible to minimize swelling.

6. Look out for symptoms of shock. Signs include a weak pulse, shallow breathing, and cold, clammy skin.

For effective examination and treatment, it is always preferable to seek the advice of a healthcare professional, especially for severe ones that require immediate medical attention.

## Life Skill #56: Treating Bug Bites and Stings

Getting bitten or stung by insects is usually minor and can easily treated at home. You might experience temporary itching, swelling, and stinging. However, certain bug bites or stings may spread disease-causing microorganisms, viruses, or parasites. Some may lead to  severe allergic reactions like anaphylaxis, especially from bees, yellow jackets, wasps, hornets, and fire ants. Here are some useful tips and techniques to help you navigate bug bites and stings.

**First Aid for Bug Bites and Stings**

1. Remove any stingers, ticks, or hair that are still embedded in the skin. Use soap and water to clean the wound.
2. For at least 10 minutes, compress any swelling with a cold compress (a flannel or towel chilled with cold water) or an ice pack.
3. Try to raise the sore spot above the level of your heart if you can.
4. Infections are less likely to occur if your fingernails are kept short and clean.
5. If you're looking for relief, old-school cures like vinegar and baking soda probably won't cut it.
6. Sometimes the discomfort, redness, and itching can linger for several days.

**Removing a Sting**

1. If you've been stung and the stinger is still in your skin, remove it immediately to stop the venom from spreading.

2. Use a credit card or something with a sharp edge to scrape it out laterally; your fingernails will do in a pinch.
3. Avoid using your fingers or tweezers to pinch the sting, as doing so may cause the release of additional venom.

**When to Get Medical Advice**

1. If you don't feel better after a few days or if your symptoms worsen.
2. If you've been stung or bitten in the face, a large (10 cm+) region of skin around the bite will turn red and swollen.
3. The pain, swelling, or redness in the area is increasing.
4. You've had a fever, swollen glands, and other signs of a systemic infection, like the flu.

## Life Skill #57: When to Head to the ER

Have you ever had that moment when you're like, "Should I head to the ER?" It's something we all ponder. But here's the deal: EMTs and paramedics work wonders, saving lives and reducing suffering at the scene and while in transit to the hospital. Depending on a patient's symptoms and the availability of resources, the ambulance may transport the patient to a facility specializing in stroke, trauma, or pediatric care.  Once you arrive, the hospital staff will sort patients by urgency. Recognizing what constitutes an ER visit is crucial for your health and safety. Here are some examples to get you thinking. If you don't see your situation on the list or are unsure, don't hesitate to call your healthcare provider.  They can provide guidance tailored to your specific circumstances. Your well-being is a priority, so reach out if you're ever in doubt.  They're your best source of advice.

**You Should Go to the Emergency Room When...**
The emergency room (ER) is intended for life-threatening or permanently disabling injuries. Potentially life-threatening symptoms that necessitate an immediate trip to the emergency room include:

1. Acute loss of vision, hearing, speech, and/or mobility.
2. Joint, muscle, or organ pain.
3. Body sagging to one side.
4. Extremely high temperature.
5. Blood in the lungs or esophagus.
6. Long-lasting convulsions (three minutes or more).
7. Breathing problems or choking.
8. Hives, swelling, and/or trouble breathing.

If you or a loved one has been in an accident or sustained serious trauma and needs immediate medical care, you should visit the nearest emergency room.

**When Should I Dial 911?**

According to the American College of Emergency Physicians, here are some instances when you should call an ambulance:

1. It looks like the person's condition is critical.
2. Relocating the victim could result in even more severe injuries.
3. The patient requires knowledge or tools available only to paramedics and EMTs.

If you or someone else is experiencing a potentially life-threatening medical emergency, call 911 right away.

# Life Skill #58: Know When to Make a Doctor's Appointment

Do I need to make an appointment with a doctor? You are not alone! Many people have wondered about this question too. Sometimes we think it is not serious enough and it will go away few days or week later. But but this is far from the truth.

According to the Centers for Disease Control and Prevention data, cough was the leading cause of medical attention sought for illness in 2023. Remember that early detection can improve the prognosis for many disorders, no matter what you are going through. Read on for guidance if you're trying to decide whether or not your condition requires medical attention.

1. **You continue to have a high fever.** The body's response to an infection is sometimes a high temperature. However, you should contact with your doctor if your temperature is over 103 degrees Fahrenheit (39.4 degrees Celsius) or if it lasts for more than three days–possible involvement of a more severe infection.

2. **Your cold gets worse**. If your symptoms persist or increase, it's time to make an appointment.

3. **You have lost weight unexpectedly and suddenly**.

4. **You are short of breath.** Common triggers for breathlessness include high altitude, vigorous exercise, obesity, and hot or cold temperatures. If you have trouble breathing and none of these seem to be the cause, you should see a doctor, especially if your symptoms come on

suddenly and severely, because you may have asthma or bronchitis.

5. **You have extreme chest, abdominal, or pelvic pain**.

6. **There has been a change in the way you urinate or pass stool.** Remember that each person's normal bowel habits are unique; therefore, the most important thing to look for is a sudden change in your pattern, such as red or black stools, diarrhea, constipation, or excessive pee. You should see a doctor if these symptoms persist.

7. **Bright flashes disrupt to your vision.** Migraine sufferers sometimes report seeing flashes of light or blind areas. A retinal detachment, a potentially blinding disorder, can manifest as abrupt, intense flashes of light outside these circumstances.

8. **You experience confusion or mood changes.** Both mental health concerns and physical conditions, such as an infection or a medicine interaction, can cause rapid changes in mood and disorientation. Watch for symptoms such as forgetfulness, inability to concentrate, disturbed sleep, and emotional ability.

9. **You think you might have a concussion.**

Check for concussion symptoms if you've hit your head or fallen on it. See a doctor if you notice any of these symptoms, including an inability to focus, headaches, irritability, and an altered sleep schedule.

**10.After undergoing a procedure or beginning a new medication, you experience unexpected side effects.** Find out from your doctor whether upcoming treatments, surgeries, vaccinations, or new drugs could have any negative consequences. Pay attention to them.

## Life Skill #59: Booking Doctor Appointments Like a Pro

Understanding what to say and do when calling for a doctor's appointment can make the process a breeze. Be prepared to offer your insurance information when you book your appointment, and have your card or other documents handy. When scheduling an appointment over the phone, remember:

1. A new patient might expect to wait a few weeks for an appointment. If you're sick and need to see a doctor ASAP, and you're already established with a primary care doctor, you can probably get an appointment the

same day you call. Alternatively, you can go to your nearest Urgent Care facility.

2. Introduce yourself and explain why you've come. You could be here because you're experiencing symptoms of a disease or disorder, such as the flu, allergies, or depression, or because you're seeking a new primary care physician(PCP).

3. Let them know whether you have health insurance or if you'll be paying out-of-pocket. Then simply tell them what health insurance policy you have.

4. Find out what, if any, documents or prescriptions you currently take need to be brought to the appointment. If you've been taking something for a while, you probably have it memorized, so you can just answer the questions.

5. Knowing a doctor's name is necessary if you wish to schedule an appointment with them. A different specialist who is available may be recommended by the office staff of your primary care physician if they are booked up and unable to see you straight away.

## Life Skill #60: Go to the Doctor on Your Own

Do you think you could handle this if it happened to you? You went to the doctor and are now back at home. But perhaps you've forgotten what your doctor instructed you to do, or you've suddenly remembered a question you intended to ask them. Whether you are starting with a new doctor or continuing to see the same doctor after many years, being prepared will help you get the most out of your session. In order to ensure that you and your doctor discuss everything that needs to be discussed, check these suggestions.

Follow these guidelines to make the most of your time in the doctor's office:

1.  **Be at your appointment 15 minutes early.** If you're a new patient seeing the doctor for the first time, getting there early will give you more time to fill out paperwork and get checked in. If you arrive early, you won't have to worry about being late.

2.  **Create a list of your questions and concerns in order of importance.** Why did you decide to come here? Do your current symptoms warrant a trip to the doctor? Do you have concerns about the medicines you're taking? Make a list of your inquiries and bring it with you. A notebook to jot down replies in can come in handy. Start with the most pressing inquiries. Do not forget that your provider probably has some questions or worries of their own.

3. **Remember to bring your prescriptions and insurance cards.** Bring your photo identification, your insurance card, and a list of the medications you are currently taking, including any dose information. Supplements and vitamins should not be left out. Bringing your current medicine or a list of your prescriptions can help your doctor avoid drug interactions.

4. **Get a friend to accompany you.** You could bring along a loved one or a friend. This person can act as a note taker and memory jogger.

5. **Update your service provider regularly.** Make sure to inform your provider of any visits you've had to other medical professionals, such as GPs, specialists, or the emergency department. Tell your doctor if you have experienced any shifts in your weight, sleep, or energy levels. There are those who keep symptom diaries.

You should also update your doctor on any changes to your family history. If you follow these guidelines, your visits to the doctor should go smoothly.

# Chapter 7

## Working World

H ave you ever been as nervous as Brian before his upcoming interview? We've all been there. Sweating through dress shirts and all, especially when it's your dream job on the line. Entering the professional world can be daunting. But with the right skills, like career searching and negotiation, you can succeed.

## Life Skill #61: Finding Your Ideal Career

Finding your ideal job path involves aligning your values and skills with your passions. Once you've got a sense of what matters to you and what you're good at, you may narrow down potential job paths. The next step is to learn as much as possible about the field you're considering entering and conduct any necessary research. Trial and error isn't something you can do before entering a field, but you can start with these nine inquiries to help you zero in on your ideal profession:

**1. What Interests You?** Instead of worrying about the type of work, the amount of money, or the required skills, center your job search on the things you enjoy doing.

**2. What are Some of Your Special Abilities?** Identify your natural abilities by answering two questions: "What do people thank you for?" Then ask, "Why do people come to you?" A career that makes good use of these abilities is possible. If you can help other people, you should be compensated for that.

**3. What Skills Do You Want to Utilize?** Making a list of your transferable skills and the most fulfilling activities will help you focus on what matters most. It's crucial to give jobs more meaning than just financial gain.

**4. What Industries are Interesting to You?** Pay close attention to your areas of interest, investigate them thoroughly, network with others working in those fields, and educate yourself on their entry points, growth opportunities, and projected future.

**5. Which Ideals Would You Most Like to Convey in Your Creations?** Doing the same thing every day makes working there worthwhile, regardless of the pay. Money is a temporary incentive; therefore, it's crucial to have something else to push you out of bed in the morning.

**6. Who are You?** Successful people understand the importance of finding a career that fits their personalities well.

**7. Where do You See Yourself Working Best?** You should prioritize your employment requirements based on company size, location, commute, people/management style, and culture.

**8. What is Your Mission?** The most crucial considerations are what aspects of your life you want highlighted in a eulogy and what drives you to action.

**9. What is Your Ideal Salary?** When making a professional shift, creating a budget that details your critical spending and any modifications you'll need to make is essential.

## Life Skill #62: Writing a Resume

A resume is a standard part of applying for jobs. Your resume is a marketing document that summarizes your experience and skills for potential employers in an organized and straightforward fashion. The point clearly states how your background and experience make you the best candidate for the job. To create a winning CV, consider the following:

**Choose the Right Format**

Select a resume format that aligns with your career history and goals. Common formats include chronological, functional, or a combination of both.

### Include Contact Information

Your name and contact details (email, phone number, LinkedIn profile URL, etc.) should be at the top of your resume.

### Include a Summary of Qualifications

Following your contact details, you can briefly explain your qualifications or a career objective statement.

### List Your Soft and Hard Skills

Think about why you're qualified for this position. Think about the technical abilities you possess, the interpersonal ones, and the transferable skills relevant to the job you're applying for.

### Include Relevant Keywords

Use relevant keywords from your work history that match with the job description to make your resume stand out. Utilize your action verbs to convey accomplishments and responsibilities effectively.

## Include a Work History

Use reverse chronological order while writing your career history section. Describe your most recent employer briefly, including the company name, the dates you were employed, your job title, responsibilities, accomplishments, and contributions.

## Include an Education Section

You may wish to include details like:

- Coursework with relevance
- Minimum 3.50 GPA
- Club and organization membership
- Positions of leadership held
- Accomplishments and professional recognition

## Think About Including Optional Sections

Use the extra space on your resume to add a list of your awards and honors, relevant certifications, volunteer work, language proficiency, and areas of interest that add value to your resume.

## Proofread and Format Your Resume.

Ensure your resume is error-free and properly formatted for a polished, professional look that is easier to read. This step is essential to keeping your potential employer interested in you.

## Life Skill #63: Job Application Process

Applying for a job might be difficult, especially if you're a teenager looking for your first employment. However, you can increase your chances of landing a job with careful preparation and attention to detail. Making a solid first impression on potential employers through your application is a proven method to stand out. Here are the easy and practical steps you should take when searching for a job.

### 1. Know Your Interests and Goals

Before you begin the application process, consider the type of job you're interested in. It could be a part-time job, a summer job, an internship, or a position related to your field of study if you're a recent graduate. What are you good at, and what kind of job would enjoy? What sort of expectations regarding work hours and pay?

### 2. Search for Job Opening in Your Field

Explore various job search resources, including job boards, company websites, and professional networks to find suitable job openings. Customize your search based on your skills, interests, and location preferences. Here are some popular job search websites:

1. https://www.indeed.com
2. https://www.glassdoor.com
3. https://www.monster.com
4. https://www.careerbuilder.com
5. https://www.simplyhired.com
6. https://www.ziprecruiter.com
7. https://www.snajajob.com
8. https://www.idealist.org
9. https://www.usajobs.gov (for U.S federal government jobs)
10. https://www.dice.com (for tech jobs)
11. https://www.flexjobs.com ( for remote and flexible job)
12. https://www.linkedin.com

## 3. Build Your Resume

Create a new resume or update one to include your contact information, education, volunteer or extracurricular activities, and skills such as computer skills, achievement, or certification. Customize it for each job application to match the job requirements.

### 4. Gather Important Documents

Gather necessary documents such as your ID, social security card, references, certificates, and transcript that may be required during the application process. You can ask your teachers, professors, or employers who know you well if they would be willing to write you references.

### 5. Fill Out Job Application

When you find a job you're interested in, fill it out accurately and completely. Pay attention to details and follow all instructions provided by the employer.

### 6. Write a Cover Letter

You can write a simple cover letter that includes an introduction about yourself, an explanation of why you are interested in the job, and any relevant skills or interests. Use a cover letter if you needed, but only if it complements your resume and offers a compelling tale.

### 6. Proofread and Edit

Review your resume, cover letter, and application for spelling and grammar errors. Attention to detail matters.

### 7. Submit Your Application

Hand in your application, including your resume, cover letter, and any request certificates or references to the employer if you are applying in person, or submit online if it's a digital application. If you copy and paste your resume into an online application, formatting errors may arise. Respond carefully to each inquiry by considering the company's interests as you do so.

**8. Application Follow-Up**

To let the employer know that you are still interested in the position, send a considerate follow-up email along with your application or call the hiring manager and ask to speak with them. It's best to give hiring managers two weeks to review resumes and applications before following up to see what happened with your application.

## Life Skill #64: Going to an Interview

One of the most critical steps in getting a job is interview preparation. Even if your qualifications and CV have called you for an interview, presenting yourself in person can really make a difference. If you're feeling anxious, that's okay. Feeling more comfortable during interviews comes with practice and experience. Here are some essential tips for a successful interview.

# 1. Research the Company

Before the interview, thorough understand the company's culture, values, mission, services, products, and recent developments. This demonstrates your genuine interest and preparedness.

# 2. Dress Appropriately

Select professional attire that suits the company culture and the position you're interviewing for.

# 3. Be on Time

The importance of punctuality can't be overstated. To respect the interviewer's time, arrive on time, ideally 10-15 minutes early.

# 4. Understand the Job Description

Carefully review the job description to identify the essential responsibilities and qualifications required. Be ready to discuss how your skills and experiences align with these requirements.

# 5. Ask Questions

Prepare some thoughtful questions to ask the interviewer to show interest in and participate in the discussion.

## 6. Practice Good Body Language

Maintain eye contact, offer a firm handshake, and sit up straight.  Positive body language demonstrates confidence and professionalism.

## 7. Maintain Positive

Avoid criticizing your experience with your school, professors, friends, or employers. The company values loyalty highly.

## 8. Address Weakness Positively

When discussing weaknesses, focus on the areas where you've made improvements or are actively working on self-development. Show our commitment to growth.

## 9. Prepare  for Behavioral Questions

Be ready to respond to  behavioral questions that evaluate how  you've handled situations in the past. Use real examples to illustrate your interpersonal problem-solving skills.

## 10. Salary Talk

Do market research on salaries beforehand to understand what your talents and expertise are worth in the current job market. But wait to bring up money or benefits until the interviewer does.

### 11. Finish on a High Note of Optimism and Energy

Don't bank on getting the job after the first interview. Try to be positive and ask what comes next. Express your enthusiasm for the position and thank the interviewer for their time. You should shake hands and smile as you leave.

### 12. Follow Up with a Thank You Note

Send a thank you email after the interview for their time, and if it's true, reiterate how interested you still are in working with them. This final action may prove pivotal. Keep it in mind.

## Life Skill #65: Getting a Reference

When looking for new employment, asking your previous employer for a reference is a good idea. The reference letter doesn't have to be long and can simply state your job title and the time you were employed. However, the reference must be reliable and fair. Your company is not allowed to make false statements about you, and they must decide what information to include in the reference in a fair manner. For instance, if a theft investigation cleared you of any wrongdoing, it would be dishonest to suggest that you were under suspicion.

## Asking Someone to be a Reference

Create a list of contacts who could serve as references. Think about people you know who would give glowing references about your skills, experience, and character. The following are acceptable citation formats:

- Counselors, professors, or tutors.
- Former managers or supervisors.
- Former employees.
- Former coworkers.
- Industry colleagues.
- Mutual acquaintances through academic or professional organizations.

## Referees Should be Informed in Advance

Notify your chosen references that you want to use them as references. This keeps them from being surprised if they are contacted.

## Ask Nicely and Gauge the Reaction You Get

Use phrasing like, "Would you be okay with being a reference for me?" to give your possible reference a choice to say no. or "I know your time is valuable; please let me know if this isn't a good time for us to talk." If they seem unsure, it's best to gently back out of the invitation and go on to the next potential guest. Maintaining the connection will benefit both parties in the future.

**Provide Them Useful Information**

Send a quick email to your references to let them know which company will contact them. Give your references a synopsis of the position you are applying for and any details you'd like them to address so they can better articulate your qualifications.

**Follow Up**

Thank your references when you've received recommendations from them. You can do this with a letter or an email that shows some consideration. Then, if you get the job, you may congratulate yourself by emailing your references to inform them that you've accepted the position and to express your appreciation for their assistance.

## Life Skill #66: Writing Professional Letters

Email is the standard for business communication nowadays. But there are still occasions when a well-written formal letter is more appropriate. Especially when you need to be professional, polite, and straight to the point, that's where it truly shines. You need to be familiar with the proper business letter to nail this. Ready to become a pro at this? Here is the guide.

## 1. List Your Address

You can skip this step by using paper with formal letterhead. If not, the upper left corner of the page is where you should put your street address, city, state, and ZIP code.

## 2. Provide the Date

Put the date just below the address.

## 3. The Recipient's Name and Address

Skip a line, then write the recipient's name and address, including their title, company or organization name, street address, city, state, and ZIP code. If you are unsure who to send your letter to, contact the organization or undertake some online research.

## 4. Professional Greeting

The usual greeting for professional letters is "Dear," while some prefer to address the recipient by name. If you don't know someone well enough to use their first name, you should address them as (Mr., Miss, Ms., Mrs., or Dr.), then their last name. If the name is unknown, use "To Whom It May Concern."

## 5. Write a Clear and Concise Subject Line

Summarize the main purpose of your message in a few words to help the recipient understand the content quickly.

## 6. Opening Paragraph

State your purpose, mention the reason for writing, and be concise. For example, in a job application email, state your interest in the position and where you found the job posting.

## 7. Body of the Letter

Break down the body of the letter into paragraphs, each addressing a specific point. *Keep it concise.*

## 8. The Closing Paragraph

Summarizing the main points express enthusiasm or appreciation and urge the reader to take action. For instance, you may remark, "Don't hesitate to get in touch with me if any further questions or concerns arise."

## 9. Closing Salutation

Place a comma and a formal sign-off after the body, such as " Sincerely," " Thank you," "Truly," and "Best Regards." Leave a signature space of four lines after the conclusion, and then sign your name.

## 10. Your Full Name

Leave a few lines for your hand written signature.

## 11. Proofread Your Work

Before sending it out, make sure it is error-free.

# Life Skill #67: Asking for a Promotion or Raise

So you have been rocking it at work, putting in the hours, and making things happen. Now, you're looking for a new position since you know you can contribute even more. But how do you bring up the topic of a raise with your boss? Is there a way to approach it without feeling awkward? Yes! Let's find out how you can kickstart that promotion conversation and recognize signs that it's time to ask for a raise.

## When to Pop the Promotion Question

- You've been doing the job for a long time, so you know what to do.
- Your job description no longer reflects your current duties.

- You've demonstrated your abilities and have the confidence to make further contributions.

## Before Asking for a Promotion

Research the job. There are numerous ways to explore the position.

- Chat with your co-worker to learn more about the job's expectations and the abilities necessary to meet those needs.

- Use online professional resources, such as publications written by industry groups, to determine what duties, responsibilities, and skills are most frequently required. These resources are already available on the website of the company you work for.

- Check out other companies with similar positions. See what skills and tasks they provide.

## Crafting Your Promotion Pitch

Your pitch is like a power-up sequence. Make sure it's got:

- Why you matter. Explain why this role is a big deal.
- Share stories of your wins to prove you're worth on display.

- Paint a picture of the awesome stuff you'll achieve in the new role.
- Admit your weak spot, but share your plan to level up those areas.

## Schedule a Time to Talk

After perfecting your pitch, it's time to meet with your boss and discuss that promotion. Consider the following points as you approach your boss about a possible promotion:

- Summarize your work experience, highlighting your most significant accomplishments and impact.
- Tell them why you want this job and what skills you'll bring.
- Describe in detail what you plan to accomplish in this position and how your contributions will benefit the company.
- Promise you're not perfect, but committed to turning your weak spots into strengths.

## Look to the Future

Regardless of the outcome, you should be pleased with yourself for taking charge of your career journey. You've got this! Remember, it's not about the promotion. It's about recognizing your value and making sure others see it, too.

# Life skill #68: Never Settle for Less Than You Deserve

Have you ever looked at your life and asked yourself whether you are truly content? Are you going after your dreams or just going with the flow? Remember, without action, it's easy to get discouraged and give up. Unfortunately, that's just the way life is sometimes. But if you want your life to be full of fire, meaning, and joy, you must train yourself to settle for nothing less than the best.

**Own Your Life**

Put an end to assigning blame and start taking responsibility for your happiness instead. Find a career you enjoy and put effort into strengthening your connection. You must take huge action to live the extraordinary life you want to create.

**Unleash Your Drive**

Those who achieve greatness always strive to improve themselves and the world around them. You can release this motivation by connecting your ambitions to a higher meaning and working toward something bigger than yourself.

**Nourish Your Body and Your Mind**

The first step in overcoming limiting ideas is to recognize them as such. Beliefs about one's future, relationships, and health that one recognizes as bad require introspection and consideration. Reigning in one's thoughts and words is crucial to overcoming self-defeating ideas. Stop saying, "I can't," and start changing your mindset to "I CAN."

## Raising Your Standards

Raising your expectations and sticking to them will allow you to use your resources, take massive action, and strengthen your convictions. Everything will start to make sense.

## Develop Success-Oriented Skills

Successful people distinguish themselves by getting up early, reading, and practicing mindfulness through yoga and meditation. Create morning rituals, imagine your perfect relationship, dream big, take action, and have faith in yourself to improve your chances of success. The secret to success and enjoying life to the fullest is found in these five methods.

# Life Skill #69: Resigning From a Job

Whether you're leaving for a better opportunity elsewhere, relocating, or for any other reason, figuring out how to quit and breaking the news can be difficult. It's essential to handle your resignation in a professional manner to maintain positive relationships with your current employer. Here is your guide on how to resign from your job gracefully and professionally:

## Determine If Now is the Appropriate Time

When leaving your employer, taking necessary steps to ensure a positive departure is essential. Consider your options carefully, converse respectfully about your resignation, wait until a new job offer is secured, and communicate your decision professionally and courteously. Remember that a positive departure can help maintain your professional reputation and increase your chances of future success.

## Give Two Weeks' Notice

Give your employer a heads-up about your departure with two week's notice. Your resignation letter should include the when and the why.

## Write a Letter of Resignation

Compose a resignation letter to the proper person to give notice:

- A formal declaration of your exit
- The date of your resignation
- A reason you are leaving
- A token of appreciation
- Your signature

**Explain Your Decision**

Talk to your human resources manager or HR person about why you're leaving your job. Set up an exit interview to leave a good impression on your previous company.

**Schedule a Time to Speak with a Manager or HR Representative**

Set up a one-on-one with your manager to discuss a strategy for completing outstanding tasks and express your gratitude for the chance to grow professionally. Create a formal resignation letter as part of your leave procedure.

**Clean Up The Loose Ends**

To facilitate a smooth transition, you should wrap up any unfinished work and keep detailed records of your daily activities for the two weeks before departing. If you're leaving to work for a rival, you should turn in any company-issued devices on the day you quit. If you are leaving for a company that is not a direct competitor, you may take any necessary equipment with you.

**Share Your Gratitude for the Opportunity**

Those who helped you get this new position should be properly thanked for their efforts.

## Life Skill #70: Managing Your Time Well

Time management is about something other than working longer or harder. It's about working smarter. Finding that balance between work and life is the key. How do you manage your time effectively and make the most of it? That's what time management is all about. Effective time management allows you to maximize your professional and personal potential. Here's how to get started:

**1. Be Mindful of Your Time Usage**

Time tracking software like "RescueTime" can help you determine how much of each day is spent on work-related tasks as opposed to pastime tasks like social media use or online shopping by using custom categories.

## 2. Stick to a Daily Schedule

Never say, "I have eight hours to do XYZ." Make yourself a daily calendar with specific time blocks for each activity.

## 3. Prioritize

Break down your to-do lists by:

- **Do immediately**: Crucial errands with specific due dates or those you've put off for far too long but now must complete.
- **Schedule for later**: Important responsibilities still need to have due dates.
- **Delegate**: Activities that can be assigned to others.
- **Delete**: Activities that aren't essential to achieving your objectives should be dropped.

## 4. Start with the Hardest Task

When your energy and focus are at their highest, start with the most difficult task first.

## 5. Group Similar Tasks

Sort the related tasks together based on their intended use to boost productivity and focus.

For example:

- Wednesday and Thursday are set aside for meetings.
- Only check your email between 10 and 11 in the morning.
- First thing in the morning, produce and send out reports.

## 6. Set Reasonable Time Limits

To prevent overworking yourself, give tasks time restrictions that are appropriate.

## 7. Learn When to Say No

Knowing your limits and being able to say no will help you avoid rushing through projects. Know your limitations and your strengths.

## 8. Avoid Multitasking

Focus on one thing at a time for better concentration and effectiveness.

## 9. Keep Things Organized

Start with the basics.

- Keep your work area tidy.
- Make sure all of your shared drives and computer folders are in sync.

- Use a calendar.

## 10. Use Time Management Tools

Make use of these time-saving and labor-saving resources:

- Slack is a messaging app used to centralize and categorize team communications via "channels."
- Use a service like Dropbox or OneDrive to back up, share, and save your files. Cloud storage allows authorized team members around-the-clock access to files.
- Outlook Calendar and Google Calendar for managing your time effectively.

# Chapter 8

## Finances and the Like

Tom's friends laughed at him when he told them he was saving for retirement when they were still teenagers. They said things like, "That's for old people" or "You plan on retiring at 40?" Little did they know, he was setting himself up for success. Tom's financial savvy became evident as the years passed while his friend struggled. Tom's early wisdom turned out to be his most brilliant move. Start your journey to financial greatness now, and prepare to take charge of your finance!

## Life Skill #71: Knowing How to Budget

Budgeting is your secret weapon for achieving spending and saving goals. It's the road map to financial independence and a stress-free life. But most people can't dive into budgeting without a solid plan. Don't worry. You can feel more confident about your financial situation and make progress toward your goals with the budget plan tailored just for you.

## Step 1: Calculate Your Net Income

Creating an intelligent budget starts with knowing how much money you get after taxes. You might be in debt if you spend based on your full salary without considering the money you take home.

## Step 2: Track Your Spending

It's vital to keep track of your expenses and organize them to understand where your money is going. This will help you identify areas where you can cut back with the least effort. When creating your monthly budget, you should break it into two categories: fixed costs (like mortgage or rent, utilities, and car payments) and variable costs (like food, transportation, and entertainment). You can keep track of money spent with a notebook, an Excel spreadsheet, or a dedicated website. In many cases, your credit card and bank statements are great sources to organize the numbers and calculate the sum of each category.

## Step 3: Set Realistic goals

Make a list of your short-term and long-term financial go to help you stay on track with your budget. Goals that are more than three years out should be considered long-term. Making and sticking to a budget is far more likely if you have specific goals.

## Step 4: Make a Plan

Set practical spending limits for different categories, considering your goals and income. Differentiate between things you want and need to make wise spending decisions. For example, expenses like gas and music subscriptions can be separated into the "needs" and "wants" categories.

## Step 5: Cut Costs to Stay Within Your Means

Reduce wasteful spending and free up cash for savings and investments by rearranging your income and expenditures. First, evaluate your "wants" to determine where to save, then analyze your regular expenses. If you're still having trouble making ends meet, it may be time to reevaluate your fixed costs. Think things out thoroughly because even a little bit of money saved can add up.

## Step 6: Review Your Budget Regularly

Maintaining financial discipline requires consistent budget and spending reviews. Examining your budget regularly is the key.

# Life Skill #72: Paying Your Bills on Time

A drop in credit score may result from late payments to creditors who report to one of the three major consumer credit bureaus. Credit card companies can charge late fees and penalty interest rates on overdue accounts. It is essential to create a strategy for bill payment. Find out what you can do to get your payments in order and stop incurring fees, interest, and damage to your credit rating.

**Make a List**

Create a master list of all upcoming payments, such as rent, mortgage, credit card, and loan installments. Create a monthly checklist using an app, spreadsheet, or notebook to record your progress. A budget can be built on the basis of this list.

**Create an Area for Paying Bills**

When bills are organized and easy to find, paying them is a breeze. Designate specific areas to store your paper and electronic bills so that you can easily locate them when it's time to pay and track which ones you've already paid.

**Check Your Statements**

If you want to prevent late fines and extra payments, you should check your invoices on a frequent basis. Keep a close eye on your bills on a regular basis to avoid fee increases. You can use this to determine if and when to reduce fees.

## Review Your Due Dates

Customers of any bank can set up email or text message alerts to serve as gentle reminders of upcoming payment dates and bill due dates. You can create a bill calendar or set up reminders on your phone when bills are due.

## Ask About Your Grace Periods

If you need more time to make a payment, a grace period of 15 days is common, but you shouldn't rely on it too heavily. You may have to request a new due date if you repeatedly use it.

## Set a Date for Paying Your Bills

Schedule a time each month, or more frequently, if necessary, when you can sit down and pay all of your payments at once. Even if you only have time to pay your bills once a month, you should make it a priority to do so.

## Simplify the Payment Process

Having the ability to schedule recurring payments through your bank or have the amount automatically deducted from your account can be a huge time and worry saver.

## Keep Paying Attention

Bills can be paid automatically, but you should still check your account balance and transactions regularly to avoid overdrafts and mistakes. It takes time and effort to set up a reliable bill-paying system, but doing so will guarantee that your payments are always paid on time.

## Life Skill #73: Being a Smart Shopper

The constant availability of advertisements for goods and services in print, television, bus shelters, storefront windows, mobile devices, and personal computers can make it hard to resist the urge to make a purchase whenever the mood strikes. These five tips can help you become a savvier consumer and should be considered before you enter your payment information online or hand over your hard-earned cash.

1. **Ask Yourself If You Need It.** This initial consideration is crucial. Intelligent consumers know exactly why they need to make a purchase. They are less likely to cave to impulses or "financial" prejudices because they are informed about the product's features, benefits, and relevance.

2. **Always Compare Prices.** The World Wide Web (www.) makes comparing prices at several stores a

breeze. You can utilize a computerized price comparison tool or check out several websites. Remember the item's regular price so you can make an informed decision about whether or not to wait for a deal like Black Friday.

3. **Take Advantage of Points or Rewards.** Smart buyers often search for discounts without compromising on quality. By enrolling in a brand loyalty program, they might save money or get better terms. They are typically for stores or brands that the customer frequently frequents. With every acquisition, you gain points redeemable for various savings, merchandise, and other incentives.

4. **Look at the Reviews.** You may learn a lot about whether a product lives up to your expectations by reading reviews before buying it. Remember that customers often leave feedback on a manufacturer's or seller's website, including information about the product's quality, customer service, problems, and faults.

5. **Make Purchases Securely.** Finally, remember to practice cybersecurity best practices when performing a financial transaction. Protect yourself by using a secure browser that begins with "https," creating strong passwords, and avoiding clicking suspicious email links.

# Life Skill #74: Building Your Savings

Saving and budgeting become much more manageable when you have a specific goal. Think of it as a road map to your dreams, whether owning a home, starting a family, or treating yourself to something you really want. So, here is what you need to know practically and stress-free.

## 1. Set Clear Savings Goals

Define why you're saving. Is it for an emergency fund, a vacation, a new car, or a down payment on a house? Having specific goals makes it easier to stay focused.

## 2. Create a Realistic Budget

It's essential to align your budget with your savings goals. One way is to allocate a portion of your income, aiming for around 20% of your paycheck, especially for savings. Review your budget and find areas where you can reduce expenses or allocate more funds to savings. It's important to be realistic about your spending habits and adjust as necessary.

## 4. Open a Teen Savings Account

Look for savings account designs for teenagers. These features might with no fees or low minimum balances and set up automated transfers to prevent spending on non-essential items. This strategy helps to develop a habit of saving and ensures you're consistently executing this skill.

## 5. Consider a Side Hustle

Explore opportunities for a side hustle or part-time job. The additional income can go directly to your savings, accelerating your progress toward your goals.

## 5. Watch Your Savings Grow

If you commit to reviewing your budget and tracking your success every month, you will be more likely to stick to your savings plan, find and fix problems promptly, and be motivated to save more money.

# Life Skill #75: Dealing with Credit Cards

When used responsibly, a credit card may be an invaluable financial instrument. Consistently paying off your accounts on schedule will help your credit score, and some cards even provide rewards for purchases or a 0% introductory APR (annual percentage rate) on balance transfers for a limited time. However, monthly payments and interest accrued might become an issue if credit spending gets out of hand. The following credit card advice will help you prevent common problems.

## Always Pay Your Monthly Balance In Full

Paying off the entire debt at the end of each billing cycle will help you avoid credit card interest. If you can control yourself and never charge more than you can afford to pay off each month, you can use a credit card interest-free. Act like your credit card is debit, and don't buy anything unless you know you have the money to pay for it. This way, you avoid interest fees.

## Use the Card for Needs, Not Wants

Credit cards can be helpful as a short-term loan in an emergency, but they should only be used sparingly to avoid getting into debt. Plan to make payments on time to minimize or eliminate interest fees.

## Never Skip a Payment

Make at least the minimum monthly payment, even if you can't afford more. If you are late with a payment, it could negatively affect your credit score and cost you money in late fees and higher interest rates.

## Leverage Credit Cards as a Budgeting Tool

Consider using a credit card to track your monthly spending. However, if you can't afford to pay off the balance every month, don't do it. Keep your credit card purchases within your means.

## Use a Rewards Card

If you use a single credit card for most of your purchases, rewards credit cards are a wise choice. While enjoying advantages like gift cards, store credit, or travel miles, you can save money on interest.

## Keep Your Credit Utilization Below 30% at All Times

The ratio of how much of your available credit you are using should be less than 30%. Ensure the total amount on all your cards doesn't exceed this threshold. Your overall utilization ratio would be 30% if you had two cards, one with a $7,000 limit and no balance and the other with a $3,000 limit and a $3,000 balance.

# Life Skill #76: Keeping Debt Under Control

With high-interest credit cards, managing debt can feel like a real struggle, making it hard to advance and reach your financial goals. However, you can take control and manage your debt better with these seven suggestions.

## 1. Account for Your Finances

Write down what you owe right now. Remember to add the interest rates for each one so you can see which ones really hurt your wallet.

## 2. Check Your Credit Report

You can request a free copy of your credit report once a year from one of the three major reporting agencies: Equifax, Experian, and TransUnion. You can order online, call, or fill out the form. Once you get the report, review it carefully to see if all the information is accurate and how debts can affect your credit.

## 3. Look for Opportunities to Consolidate

Pay off credit card debt by taking out a low-interest personal loan or consolidating high-interest loans into one. Before consolidating or refinancing, determine if you qualify for federal loan forgiveness programs.

## 4. Be Honest About Your Spending

If you are having trouble making ends meet due to excessive debt, look honestly at your monthly expenditures. Is there anything you could do without or reduce to help with the tight finances? Limiting new borrowing is one of the many necessary steps to reduce debt.6nuh

## 5. Determine How Much You Have to Pay

If you have multiple debts, consolidate them by noting the minimum payments and adding the amount to a budget. Make contact with creditors and negotiate new arrangements.

## 6. Consider How Much More You Can Afford to Spend

Find out how much extra you can put toward paying off debt, with the expectation that doing so will free up some spending cash in the future.

## 7. Plan Out How You'll Get Out of Debt

The most common ways to tackle debt is to pay off the accounts with the highest interest rates first, followed by those with the lowest interest rates.

# Life Skill #77: Building Your Credit Score

Building credit is a step-by-step process that requires patience and discipline. It is like having a report card for your financial skills. To get started, you have to get some credit accounts. These accounts act as your financial storytellers and report to credit bureaus, informing them about how responsible you are with your money. Using credit wisely and paying off balances on time will help you progressively establish a solid credit history and raise your credit score.

## 1. Start with Credit Accounts

Get a credit card or consider a small loan to initiate your credit history.

## 2. Understand the Score

Your credit score is like your financial GPA. Aim for 700 or above, equivalent to receiving an A+ in the credit game.

## 3. Responsibility is Key

Only spend what you can afford to pay back.

## 2. Pay on Time

Making all of your payments on time is crucial if you want to have good credit. Contact credit card companies to discuss hardship options, set up automated payments for the minimal amount owing, and monitor accounts not reflected on credit reports.

## 3. Pay Off Overdue Bills

If you need to catch up on your obligations, doing so will enhance your credit score and encourage you to stay caught up.

## 4. Reduce Outstanding Credit Card Debt

Keeping balances low compared to available credit will help revolving credit scores. High-credit-score individuals use less than 10% of their available credit.

## 5. Limit the Frequency of Account Opening Requests

To avoid damaging your credit ratings, space out your credit application submissions. When you're applying for credit cards or loans all at once, lenders think you are in some financial trouble. So spread out your application over time to look more responsible and better for your credit score.

# Life Skill #78: Filing Your Taxes

Completing your federal income tax return may seem daunting at first. But if you break it down into manageable steps, you may save money and avoid making beginner mistakes during tax season. Here is a quick reference for filing and getting your taxes done quickly and easily.

## 1. Keep Track of Your Income

As of 2022, anyone earning over $12,950 a year and meets the IRS's minimum threshold must file a tax return in the United States. Include all the earnings from your jobs and any other revenue resource, such as investments, dividends, and interest.

## 2.  Keep Relevant Records Throughout the Year

Keep your financial data organized all year. Save all receipts linked to gifts, purchases, medical expenses, loan and investment statements, and other income records.  More importantly, make sure you keep receipts from donations throughout the year.  These will be deducted from your taxes. When tax season begins, keeping these records will save you time.

## 3.  Collect Necessary Documents

Gather these forms like W-2s and 1099-NECs for deductions and credits for tuition and fees. Form 1098-T for dividend, interest, and student loan interest statements.  So ensure you have them handy because they are key to effectively computing deductions and credits.

## 4. Choose Your Filing Status

Determine your filing status. Most teens will file as single or dependent on their parent's tax return.

## 5. Find Out Which Tax Breaks and Deductions You Qualify for

You can save time and effort compiling the necessary paperwork if you know the possible credits and deductions for which you qualify. Some examples are as follows:

- **Saver's credit**. You could be eligible for a tax credit if you contribute to a retirement plan depending on your tax filing status and AGI.
- **Student loan interest**. Depending on your MAGI after adjustments, you may deduct interest payments totaling up to $2500.
- **Charitable deductions**. Putting money toward your alma mater or a cause you care about. You can usually deduct money you gave to a charity that meets specific requirements if you itemize your taxes.
- **Freelance expenses**. Expenses like professional memberships and office supplies may be tax deductible for the self-employed.

## 6. Mind Your Deadlines

The easiest way to avoid identity theft and get your tax refund quickly is to file your forms as soon as possible. The deadline for submitting federal income tax returns in U.S is April 15th, but it may change annually.

## 7. Choose Your Tax Filing Method

Choose between filing on paper or electronically. Filing online is often quicker and can help avoid common errors. However, you can file your taxes in many different ways.

- **Free File:** The Internal Revenue Service provides free tax software to aid in filing tax returns.

- **IRS online forms**: The IRS provides electronic forms to assist in determining adjusted gross income; however, they only give the basic instructions.

- **Tax preparation software:** It is possible to find and claim more tax breaks and credits with the help of online resources.

- **Tax preparer:** Make sure you use a reliable tax preparer by consulting the IRS's official database of tax preparers who have passed background checks.

## Life Skill #79: Paying Your Taxes

In the past, taxpayers who owed money to the IRS ( Internal Revenue Service) had to send in checks. Nowadays, there are many other options available that are more secure and convenient. The IRS recommends using Direct Pay, EFTPS ( Electronic Federal Tax Payment System) , or a credit or debit card to pay your taxes online rather than sending a check in the mail. With these tax payment options, you can choose the best method for you and make an informed decision.

**Direct Pay**

Direct pay allows you to transfer funds directly from your bank account to the IRS. There are no service fees. The payment date can be adjusted or canceled up to two business days before the planned payment date, and payments can be made as far in advance as 30 days.

## Electronic Fund Withdrawal

You can pay your taxes through EFW; however, there can be a fee. You can arrange it up to a year in advance, but only if you e-file your federal taxes.

## Electronic Federal Tax Payment System

One of the most straightforward methods is the Electronic Federal Tax Payment System (EFTPS). Only those with a valid SSN or ITIN, PIN, internet password, and secure browser can make payments. The enrollment process might take up to five days, and payments may be made up to a year in advance.

## Credit and Debit Card

Payments made to the IRS via debit or credit card over the phone or online are not subject to a fee. Payment options include major credit cards and alternatives like PayPal and PayNearMe.

## Check or Money Order

You can pay your tax bill to the IRS using a check or money order. You must submit form 1040-V along with your payment. Send the complete package to the address listed on the back of the form.

**Cash**

You can pay tax in cash, but don't try to mail it in! A bank or retail outlet that handles money transactions is where you need to be. This can be done at the IRS's Taxpayer Assistance Centers (TACs), and at many major convenience stores and pharmacies.

## Life Skill #80: Saving for Retirement

Planning for retirement may seem like a far-off goal, but starting early can turn it into a reality and potentially have a comfortable one. Saving for retirement is a long-term journey. But if you begin putting money away earlier rather than later, the amount saved for retirement is something you can work on improving. You can start saving for retirement at any point in your life, so consider the following suggestions to help you reach your savings goals.

**Focus on Starting Today**

Compound interest allows assets to generate earnings, which may be reinvested to create even more; thus, it's essential to start saving as soon as possible. The earlier you start, the more time your money has to grow.

## Contribute to Your 401(k) Account

Take advantage of 401(k) plan offered by your employer. Contributions are often made pre-tax, which might lower your current tax bill.  If your company offers a Roth 401(k), consider a Roth 401(k), particularly when you expect to be in a higher tax bracket after retirement.

## Meet Your Employer's Match

If your company offers a 401(k)-matching program, it's in your best interest to contribute at least enough to receive the entire match. It's free money for your retirement.

## Open an IRA

Opening a traditional IRA or a Roth IRA is a good idea to save for retirement. However, Traditional IRA contributions may be tax deductible. Roth IRA contributions  are made after-tax dollars, and any earnings are distributed tax-free upon retirement.  You can start one with an investment banking service such as Morgan Stanley or Charles Schwab.

## Make "Catch-Up" Contributions at 50+

The amount you may put into a retirement account or a 401(k) each year is capped, so it's important to start early and take advantage of the maximum annual contribution limit for retirement accounts and 401(k). You can make catch-up contributions when you are over 50, boosting your retirement savings. Take advantage of  this opportunity to secure your financial future.

## Automate Your Savings

Set up a recurring monthly payment to your retirement fund to make saving for retirement easier, and your savings may increase without you having to give it any thought.

## Cut Costs

Check your spending habits and see where to save more money for retirement. It's possible to save money by carrying a packed lunch to work rather than buying it or by negotiating a lower rate on your auto insurance.

## Set a Goal

The act of saving can be more satisfying if you clearly know how much you could need in the future. Motivate yourself as you work toward your retirement objective by setting intermediate goals.

## Stash Extra Funds

It's important to be aware of your shopping habits. One strategy to assure financial security is to raise the percentage of your salary that you put into retirement each time you get a raise. Put at least fifty percent of the windfall into your 401(k) or other retirement fund. If you get additional money, such as a tax refund or a work bonus, consider putting at least fifty percent of the windfall into your 401 (k) or retirement account. Avoid using it to buy unnecessary luxuries or go on an unnecessary vacation.

## Consider Deferring Collecting Social Security s Retirement Nears

Social Security retirement benefits can be started as early as 62 but will be decreased if received before the full retirement age (age 67 for those born after 1960). If you can wait until you're 70, you'll receive a greater monthly benefit and more money throughout your lifetime. Even delaying retirement by a single year could have a significant impact.

# Chapter 9

# Survival Skills 101

I n middle school, David read the book "Hatchet" and found himself in a real-life survival scenario during a camping trip. With no smartphone or GPS, he had to rely on his knowledge of wilderness survival from adventure novels. Could he navigate through dense wood and build a fire without a lighter? How can he find safe drinking water and distinguish it from the harmful kind? Can he identify edible plants and hunt for food? As a teen, he was about to put his reading to the test, and in this chapter, we are going to equip you with these crucial survival skills just in case you ever find yourself on a wilderness adventure.

## Life Skill #81: Building a Fire

The ability to start a fire without using matches or a lighter is crucial in times of need. You never know when you might find yourself in a jam that requires fire. Knowing how to build a fire in an old-fashioned manner is a terrific party trick to amaze anybody you take camping, even if you don't want to venture too far from civilization on your road trip. Here is a basic guide to help you ignite a fire without resorting to matches or a lighter.

## The Hand Drill

1. **Gather Materials.** Collect the necessary materials, including a dry, flat piece of wood for the fireboard, a long, straight stick for the drill, and some dry tinder-like leaves or grass.

2. **Prepare the Fireboard.** Carve a slight depression or notch in the fireboard. This is where the ember will form. Make a V-shaped groove leading from the board's edge to the notch.

3. **Create the Drill.** Use the straight stick as your drill. It should be about the thickness of your thumb and roughly 2 feet long. Sharpen one end to a point.

4. **Build a Tinder Nest.** Gather some dry leaves, grass, or other fine, easily ignitable material to create a tinder nest. Place this below the V-shaped notch on your fireboard.

5. **Start Drilling.** Place the pointed end of your drill into the depression on the fireboard. Hold the drill between your hands and start rolling it rapidly back and forth. Apply downward pressure to create friction. This will generate heat and create an ember in the notch.

6. **Ignite the Tinder.** Carefully transfer it to your tinder nest as a glowing ember form in the notch. Gently blow on

the ember to encourage it to ignite the tinder. Once it starts burning, carefully place it under your prepared firewood to build your campfire.

## Fire Plow

All you need is a tougher wood for the plow and a softer wood for the plow board. Plow boards are best made of willow or poplar.  It would be beneficial for you to learn how to identify different trees as well, especially knowing hardwoods versus softwoods!

1. Prepare your hearth by cutting a groove six to eight inches long and one inch wide down the board. Locate a piece of hardwood approximately a foot long and chisel off the end so that it points.
2. Put the plow's head on the fireplace screen. Start rubbing the plow's point back and forth in the middle of the grove. The result will be pinpoint dust depressions.
3. The board must be raised. Raise the board's upper edge and rest it on your knee to channel dust to the lower surface.
4. Accelerate the pace. If you wait until a mound of dust forms at the bottom, you won't be able to stoke the fire with the plow.

5. Bring the fire to the tinder. After the dust has caught fire, you can move it to the tinder and start a fire by gently blowing on it. Be careful not to blow it out!

## Life Skill #82: How to Chop Wood

Not only is learning how to chop wood cool, but it's also incredibly useful and environmentally friendly. Wood knowledge is a significant advantage, whether relaxing at home or adventuring in the wilderness. Imagine yourself outside and requiring a fire for cooking and warmth. You can't just click your fingers and make it happen, can you? To cut wood is to open the natural heating system. Furthermore, it is a hidden superpower that extends from the forest to the stove and is not only about warmth. Wood chopping appeals to those who value sustainability and physical labor. Prepare yourself for the wood-chopping adventure! It will be practical, cool, and somewhat like an outdoor hero.

**Methods for Efficiently Chopping and Stacking Firewood**

If you want to get the most out of your wood, you should:
1. Chop some trees in the winter, then dry them up in the summer. The drying process typically takes two years.

2. Reduce the length of the planks. The drying time for short pieces is less than that for long ones. Logs lose 10–15% more moisture through their ends than through their lengths.

3. When chopping wood, try to expose as much surface area as possible. Bark acts as a barrier, enclosing whatever moisture it encounters. It is easier for water to evaporate from logs if more of their surfaces are exposed. Additionally, wood that has been chopped into appropriate-sized pieces is more efficient in the wood-burning stove.

## Wood Chopping, Step-By-Step

1. Spread your legs far apart and stand tall.
2. Throw the ax over your back or behind your head.
3. Maintain an open stance.
4. The ax should be swung with the hand closest to the head.
5. You need only slide down the shaft of the handle.
6. Before you make a strike, it could be helpful to bend your knees slightly.
7. Being quick on your feet helps you finish the job.
8. Don't think twice about it; make the cut.

# Life Skill #83: Navigating in the Wild

Even if your phone is your go-to navigator, having compass skills is useful when you're out in the wild. Once you spot north on your map, the other directions fall into place. You can then use your compass to point in the direction you wish to travel. Your compass is invaluable for finding your way, whether you're lost or at a crossroads.

## Master the Use of the Compass and Its Components.

A compass's symbols, numbers, and letters might initially confusing. Understanding the cardinal directions is crucial. We'll walk you through key features like the index line, bezel, magnetic needle, orientation lines, and direction arrow.

## Turn the Bezel

The compass's bezel is like your steering wheel. You can turn it to adjust its orientation. Rotate the compass's bezel until the arrow points in the desired direction. You're free to head in any direction, but the four cardinal points make an excellent place to begin. The yellow circle in this example indicates that we will choose E for east. It helps to start N for North, though, because in a clockwise sequence, the compass is N, E, S, and W. You can remember the order because W and E are L & R.  It spells WE.  Look for the "we" to orient your direction.  Then N and S are just above and below, which are in alphabetical order!

**Align the Magnetic Needle**

The floating part of a compass is the magnetic needle. Keeping the compass flat in front of you at right angles to your body, turn until the red tip of the floating magnetic needle falls within the orienting lines (or arrow).  Once you have found "we",  you can now orient yourself.

**Walk In Your Desired Direction**

First, you'll need to line up your compass and choose a point to walk to ahead of you in the direction it is pointing. Once you have your bearings, you can set out on foot. You can walk straight if you keep the magnetic arrow within the orienting lines. However, it is impractical to check the compass constantly. Choose a prominent landmark up ahead in the direction your compass indicates you should travel. Proceed to that location, where you can reorient your compass and decide where to go.

**What If You Don't Have a Compass?**

Navigating the wild without a compass can be challenging but doable with a few handy tips.

As you move around, create your landmarks by marking trees or rocks to help you find your way back. If you come across a stream or river, following it downstream will often lead you to civilization. Use the sun to your advantage. The sun rises in the east and sets in the west. If you know the time of the day, you can figure out directions based on where the sun is. Take notes of other natural features like mountains, rivers, or distinctive trees. Use them as reference points to guide your direction. Also, pay attention to the patterns in the landscape, such as the slope of hills, valleys' shape, and vegetation's growth pattern.

When it comes to nighttime, the most dependable compass is above your head, the North Star or Polaris. Just look for the brightest star in the sky to find it. It is helpful gauge to measure the distance between the North Star and your thumb when your middle finger is fully extended.

## Life Skill #84: Locating and Purifying Water

Knowing how to find and purify water is a crucial survival skill, especially when you're out in the wilderness. You never know when unexpected situations might arise, and having access to clean water is essential for your well-being. Being resourceful and knowing where to locate safe drinking water is a skill that can make a big difference whether you're hiking, sightseeing, or exploring.

## Locating Water

When you're looking for water in the wild, you can do a few things to increase your chances of finding it. One is to follow animal trails as they often lead to water sources. You can also listen for the sound of running water or look for lush, green vegetation, which usually indicates the presence of water. Exploring valleys and the base of the hills is also a good idea, as water typically flows to lower ground. If you notice damp soil or seepage, using a stick to dig a shallow hole can reveal water. Observing bird flight patterns or insects like bees and mosquitoes can also point to water resources.

## Purifying Water

When you find water in the wild, the water might not be clear and safe to drink. In emergency situations, knowing how to purify water effectively for drinking is crucial. You can fashion a makeshift filter using a large container, a hollow piece of wood, or a plastic bag. A Hollow bamboo can also serve the purpose. Make five to ten holes in the container's bottom, and then suspend it from those holes. Layer the container with rocks, sand, and fabric alternately. The more layers you incorporate, both fine and coarse, the more effective the filtration. Pour the collected water into the filter, accumulating the filtrate in a separate container. If the water remains unclear after the initial filtration, consider running it through the filter again for added purification.

## Life Skill #85: Identifying Poisonous Plants

Your backyard might be full of memories, but have you checked for any dangerous plants? The old nursery rhyme "Leaves of three, leave them be" is a good starting point for learning to identify poison ivy and oak so you can avoid the unpleasant symptoms they cause. As beautiful as they are, many ornamental plants and flowers are not meant for snacking. Here are some plants that you should keep an eye out for:

**Common poisonous plants**

**1. Poison Ivy**

This plant is widespread throughout the United States. It tends to climb or form a little bush. It has three glossy leaves, each of which may be a different color depending on the time of year. If touched, it can be irritating to the skin and it will linger for days.

## 2. Poison Oak

Like poison ivy, it can be either a vine or a small shrub. Its symptoms include itching, redness, and occasionally blistering.

## 3. Poison Sumac

Poison sumac is more dangerous than poison ivy and poison oak but is far less frequent. This poisonous plant has been known to induce rashes and swelling if touched.

## 4. Castor Oil Plant

Contrary to its usefulness as a landscape plant, this species' oil seeds are extremely poisonous to people and animals. Severe nausea, vomiting, diarrhea, and dehydration could be the results. Kidney and liver failure, and not to scare you, but even death can be a result.

## 5. Giant Hogweed

The maximum height of this invasive plant is 14 feet. When exposed to sunlight, the sap from this plant can inflict severe burns and scarring.

## 6. Water Hemlock

With its tiny white blooms, this bush is sometimes a noxious weed along streams and moist meadows. It's extremely poisonous and has a distinct carrot aroma. It's highly toxic and affects the nervous systems of animals and people.

# Life Skill #86: Foraging Mushrooms

Venturing into the woods for wild mushrooms can be like a natural treasure hunt. It's an enjoyable pastime that can earn you extra pocket money. However, not all mushrooms are edible, and some can be toxic. Therefore, knowing which mushrooms are safe to eat and which should be avoided is valuable.

## Use Apps and Books

Wild Edibles is only one of many applications that can help you identify edible mushrooms in the wild. If you're not the app type, pack some books and head out into the wilderness.

## Cut, Don't Pull

It's better to cut the mushrooms than to try to pull them up by their roots. When the roots are yanked up, the plant dies. Next year, you should expect to see cut mushrooms again.

## Gather What You Need

Sustainable mushroom foraging requires taking only as many as you can use. Mushrooms are permissible if you intend to put them in a container and consume them later. But pick only a small amount at a time so the mushrooms have time to recover.

## Take Pictures and Seek Advice

Join some online communities dedicated to mushroom hunting where you can share photos for identification purposes. Next time you're out and about and come across a mushroom you're unfamiliar with and want to avoid picking, pull out your phone and snap a photo. One aspect of mushroom hunting involves drawing on the expertise of seasoned fungi enthusiasts.

## Forage After a Heavy Rain

After a rainstorm, the woods will be the perfect environment for mushroom growth because of the increased moisture and humidity. Following a drought, they explode in growth following a good rainstorm.

## Learn Where to Look for Mushrooms

The most challenging aspect of mushroom foraging is locating the fungi. However, there are specific conditions and locations where various mushroom varieties thrive. Watch for fallen logs or stumps, as some mushrooms love to grow on decomposing debris. Check around the root zone and the vicinity of tree trunks for plant species that thrive there. Explore recently burned areas of woods or fields can be fruitful as the mushroom forest grows in a scorched landscape. Additionally, mushrooms love loamy soil, which consists of sand, clay, and organic material, making such areas a hotspot. Don't forget to look beside streams and creeks. The high moisture content provides an ideal environment for these mushrooms to thrive.

## Familiarize Yourself with Poisonous Mushrooms

It's essential to be able to recognize edible mushrooms apart from their poisonous ones. Proper identification can prevent mistaking a death cap mushroom as a tasty treat.

## A Warning

Never consume a mushroom you can't be sure about its safety.

# Life Skill #87: Finding Berries

Finding berries can be a tasty and helpful skills when you're out in the wild. There are many different types of wild berries that you may encounter on a foraging trip, some of which you can eat. However, being cautious is essential because a berry is edible, but it doesn't mean the whole plant is safe. Some wild berries can only be eaten after being cooked, while others have edible fruit but inedible seeds or leaves.

**Identify Edible Wild Berries**

Berries are a good source of carbohydrates, fiber, and vitamins. Here are a few guidelines for evaluating whether or not you can eat the berries you've found in the wild.

- **Textured Skin is a Good Sign**. Thimbleberries, mulberries, raspberries, and salmonberries are all examples of aggregate berries, which are characterized by their dense clusters. They have bumpy skin made up of many particles. These berries are ninety-nine percent edible worldwide and usually won't require an edibility test (though it never hurts to check).

- **Blue, Black, and Purple Skin is a Trust Worthy Factor**. Black, purple, and blue-skinned berries have a 90 percent chance of being edible. One notable exception to this rule is the nightshade berry, which looks deceptively similar to a blueberry but is toxic. You should strongly consider an edibility test before consuming berries that have blue, black, or purple skin.

- **Orange and Red are 50/50**. Orange and red berries are more likely to be harmful than dark-skinned berries. These berries have a fifty-fifty chance of being edible, so you always want to perform an edibility test before consuming them.

- **Avoid Green, White, and Yellow Berries**. These berries are the most like poisonous and should be avoided when possible. With only ten percent of them edible, these berries have the highest risk of toxicity.

## Edible wild berries

1. Blackberries
2. Blueberries
3. Cloudberries
4. Cranberries
5. Elderberries
6. Gooseberries
7. Huckleberries
8. Raspberries
9. Serviceberries
10. Wild strawberries

## Poisonous wild berries

1. Baneberries
2. Bittersweet nightshade
3. Holly berries
4. Horse Nettle fruit
5. Ivy berries
6. Mistletoe berries
7. Nightshade
8. Pokeweed berries
9. Virginia creeper berries
10. Yew berries

## Life Skill #88: Finding Other Wild Edibles

You can pick up a wild edible plant in any direction. Eating wild plants is a significant step toward self-sufficiency in the woods, and it's free. Whether you intend on making a meal out of free greens or want to taste some new flavors on your next camping trip, you'll be prepared once you learn where to look and how to prepare plants you find in the wild. If eaten in excess, the wrong plant might be lethal. Safety first!

### Tips

Bear in mind that if you reside in a particularly humid area, most of your foraging opportunities will be best served by seeking out the sunniest clearing or "edge" in the forest. Most of the wild food in a dry area, like the Southwest of the United States, will be found in or near water.

Get a copy of a plant atlas for your area. Find out how to identify and prepare your area's most common "weeds" (also known as edible plants) in your area. Study the top 20, or even 25, and commit them to memory; you never know when you might need them.

Your lawn is an excellent location to start looking for wild food plants. Wild onion, violets, dandelion, wood sorrel, chickweed, plantain, henbit, clover, dead nettle, and sow thistle are all completely edible weeds that can flourish in routinely removed areas. Depending on where you reside or what you forage for, some may go by different names.

Don't try eating grass; not all types are edible. It's easy to chew and digest food that's less than six inches long. Anyone who has tried a shot of wheatgrass knows how delicious it can be, but the flavor may range from incredibly sweet to moderate to harsh. You can manually juice wheatgrass longer than 6 inches or simply chew it and spit it out.

Go somewhere else that gets cleaned up frequently. Fields, parks, and the like are all good options. There will be a plethora of food plants there as well. You can gather chickweed by the bucketload. What you should search for is:

1. Dead-nettle
2. Wood Sorrel
3. Henbit
4. Sow thistle
5. Plantain
6. Dandelion
7. Chickweed
8. Wild onion
9. Cress

**Other tips**

1. Look for plants that grow in wet areas.
2. Find fruiting trees.
3. Find deciduous leaves ( you should've already learned something about this in the identifying tree section!).
4. In the spring, collect the young needles from conifers.
5. Get familiar with grapevines so you can tell them apart.
6. Nibble on safe flowers.
7. Check out the thorny brambles for food.
8. Look for berries on ornamental shrubs.
9. Look for berries on trees.
10. Check out the lofty trees.

11. Look for nuts beneath the trees.

# Life Skill #89: How to Swim

On a warm summer day, nothing beats a refreshing swim. Swimming, though, is a lifesaving skill in its own right. Learning to swim is a prerequisite for participating in water sports like kayaking and surfing. One of the best forms of exercise is swimming. Your muscles, heart, and lungs will all benefit from working harder than usual. Taking swimming classes is your best bet for learning how to swim.

**How to Do Breaststroke**

1. Put your face down and float horizontally with your body straight. Keep your hands together and your arms and legs at your sides.
2. Make a "thumbs down" gesture. Raise your elbows and circle your hands out and back. Raise your head and take a deep breath.
3. Hold your hands together, thumbs pointing up, in front of your shoulders. Maintain a close grip on your elbows. Bring your feet up toward your buttocks while pointing them outward and bending your knees.

4. Extend your arms in front of you. Snap your feet together and then kick out and back in a circle. Submerge your head and let out a deep breath.

5. Glide forward and repeat.

## How to Do a Butterfly

1. Keep your head above water and your body horizontal while you float. Keep your hands together and your arms and legs at your sides.

2. Position your head forward and down and your hips high. The next step is to lift your chin and squat down. Keep going back and forth like a wave.

3. If you drop your head, you should kick with your hips. Put your hands past your hips and extend your arms. Raise your head and breathe in at the same time.

4. Kick and carry on the body wave by raising your arms above your head and across the water. Submerge your head and then your arms. Exhale. This finishes one rotation of the arm.

5. Every two or three breaths, take a deep one.

## How to Do Freestyle

1. Keep your head underwater and your body horizontal while you float. Put your hands together and maintain a long, lean posture.

2. To do a flutter kick, alternately raise and lower one foot. Quickly switch between the two while maintaining a flexible ankle and knee.

3. Extend your right hand forward, palm down, about 12 to 18 inches, in a position aligned with your shoulder.

4. Bring it down and back with your right hand so that your fingers are pointed diagonally down. Raise your elbow to the sky.

5. Raise your right hip and shoulder as your right hand reaches your thigh. Raise your hand above the surface and across the water.

6. Put your right hand in the water, then your left, and so on.

7. Take a deep breath every two or three strokes when your hand leaves the water.

## Life Skill #90: How to Hunt

Hunting is a serious skill that requires patience, know-how, and an in-depth understanding of the natural world. It goes beyond simply catching animals. It's about respecting the balance of life in the wilderness. Before you embark on hunting journey, gathering     proper     knowledge     and preparation is crucial. Here is a step-by-step guide to kickstarting your hunting journey.

## Step 1. Decide on Your Preferred Game

Making a prey selection is the first step in hunting. In that regard, it's like choosing your crazy journey. Are you interested in going rabbit, duck, or deer hunting? Maybe you prefer to shoot wild boar, birds, or the beautiful elk. While always bearing in mind ethical and appropriate hunting tactics, factors like the location, the season, and your own preferences will have an impact on your choice.

## Step 2. Research Effective Hunting Tools

The right hunting equipment must be understood and acquired. Your decision on a weapon will depend on the type of game you intend to shoot as well as any applicable local laws. Whether you use a rifle, bow and arrow, shotgun, or black powder gun, make sure you understand safe gun handling before asking experienced hunters for guidance. Just as it is important to have a deep grasp of your prey, having a good understanding of your gear is a crucial part of ethical hunting.

## Step 3. Learn Some Strategies for Hunting the Game You Want

There are many ways to use it, depending on what you are after and where you are. If you prefer to move covertly, choose "Sport and Stalk" or "Still Hunting." It's like sneaking patiently and stealthily through the woods like a ninja.

You might choose the traditional "Ambush" tactic, which entails laying up a trap for your target while observing them from a concealed blind or from a tree stand. If you've got a gift for gab, "Calling" is your jam. To mislead predators or ducks into approaching, you imitate animal sounds.

People who enjoy working as a team will enjoy "Driven Hunt," where you and your friends coordinate to push the game toward waiting hunters. It is similar to a tactical mission. Dogs can make ideal hunting partners. They act as your wingmen, assisting you in "Flushing" wildlife out of the cave or "Hunting with Dogs" for more varied hunting.

Try " High-Seat Hunting" for a bird's-eye perspective while sitting on a tree or tower. Alternatively, use "Decoying" creatively by placing false animals to draw genuine ones. If you like "Tracking," you can locate them by looking for hints that animals have left behind. "Bowhunting" is for people who enjoy a close-up challenge, but "Rife Hunting" is similar to taking a precise shot from a far distance.

Some hunters use specialized tools like crossbows and muzzleloaders to up the ante. With the aid of dogs and decoys, "Upland Bird" and "Waterfowl Hunting" are focused mainly on birds. Rabbits, squirrels, and other small game are the focus of "Small Game Hunting." "Night Hunting" focuses on nocturnal animals. While "Trapping' is similar to putting puzzles in front of the game. "Calling and Decoying Predators" is somewhat like pulling pranks on the cunning animals.

## Step 4. Prepare for the Hunt

Before heading out, ensure all your equipment is in working order and you have all the essential items.

1. Get permission, if necessary
2. Check weather conditions
3. Check your gear
4. Gather supplies, such as:
   - Waterproof cell phone or two-way radio
   - Dress in layers and bring rain gear, just in case
   - Lighters/fire starters
   - Survival knife
   - Waterproof light source (e.g., headlamp)

- Whistle or signaling device
- Metal cup
- Emergency shelter (e.g., space blanket)
- First aid kit
- Food bars, granola, and other emergency supplies
- Map and compass
- Put together emergency supplies
- Supplemental medications (insulin, blood pressure medicines, etc.) that must be taken every day

## Step 5. Hone Your Skills

Honing your hunting skills requires continuous learning and practice. You can improve your hunting skills by engaging in the following techniques:

1. Practice shooting from different positions, such as standing, kneeling, and prone. Work on accuracy and precision.
2. Target shooting at various distances
3. If you are into bowhunting, practice archery, work on draw, aim, and release.
4. Familiarize yourself with the terrain. Before season starts, take some time to scout your hunting ground

and look for signs of animal activity, such as game trails, tracks, and droppings.

5. Practice moving silently through the surrounding area using camouflage and stealth.

6. Practice mimicking the animal sounds

7. Study animal tracking and sign language. Learn to recognize game trails and follow animal footprints.

8. Practice a variety of hunting tactics in different hunting scenarios.

9. Hunting with experienced hunters and observing their methods, approaches, and choices

## Step 6. Begin to Hunt

It's time to start the hunt. The game you're playing and any geographical restrictions will determine this. If you plan on hunting deer in the evening, you might want to go to your stand by 3 or 4 o'clock in the afternoon.

# Chapter 10

## The World of Dating

W ill is a regular adolescent boy. For the past six months or so, he has been crushing on Samantha. Their eyes would always meet in the school hallways, and a lovely grin exchange would occur.

However, he is faced with a small problem. Samantha has never actually been approached by Will, and initiated the conversation. Yes, even the finest of us experience it. The whole "what do I say?" situation can be challenging.

Don't worry if you have ever been in Will's position or if you currently find yourself in it. On your side, we are. In this lesson, we'll explore the art of making eye contact with that particular someone, having memorable discussions, and turning smiles into memories. The entire dating process is essential, not just the asking-out process. So let's do this!

## Life Skill #91: Asking a Girl Out on a Date

Working up the courage to ask a girl out on a date can be challenging. You can't predict if she'll say no to your invitation or yes. You'll be worried about how you come across physically, verbally, and emotionally. But with the proper approach, you can enhance your chances of success.

## Communicating Your Interest

Ask her out in person, but you need to do it right. Don't approach her when she's preoccupied or not paying attention. It's important to find the right moment. Avoid jumping the gun and asking too soon into a conversation. Focus on getting to know her better. Engage in casual conversation and seek small talk opportunities, like while waiting in line or during breaks. It's important to pay attention to her likes and dislikes, make sure to take note of them. Make eye contact, as it conveys genuine interest. Build a connection, engage in meaningful dialogue, and take that step when the time is right. This way, you'll increase your chances of a positive response and make the experience enjoyable for both of you.

## Plan the Date

Clarity is vital when planning a date. Don't leave each other guessing; it's better to be precise. Make sure you decide on a specific time that works for both of you and define a particular location. Inform her about your plans, including where you'll be going and what activities you'll be doing, so she can prepare accordingly. Being upfront and organized shows that you're considerate, which makes the whole experience smoother and more enjoyable.

## Asking Her Out

When it's time to make your move, ensure you're dressed neatly and approach her when she's alone for a comfortable conversation. Be confident, and keep things light and upbeat. It sets a good vibe. Show your interest by asking questions, but don't get too nosy. When the moment feels right, invite her with a friendly tone and a smile. If she says no, it's okay; she might have a reason. Ask if there's a better time for her. Be cool and keep things friendly if it's a clear no. It's a learning experience. But if she says yes, great! Wrap up the conversation smoothly and start planning that date. Remember, respect, confidence, and staying positive are keys to dating.

## Treating Her Right

Respecting and being kind to your date is the basis of a solid and meaningful connection. To achieve this, actively listen to your date, respect her boundaries, and prioritize consent.

Take the time to get to know her interests without jumping to judgment. You must be reliable and keep your promises to show your trustworthiness. Go above and beyond to surprise her with thoughtful gestures to make her feel appreciated. Balancing your personal life and relationships with dating is crucial to respecting individuality and fostering growth. If any concerns or issues arise, address them openly and calmly. In dating, respect, kindness, and communication form the bedrock of a positive foundation.

**Follow-Up**

You can send her a thoughtful follow-up text the day after your first encounter, keeping it concise and direct. You can express that you had a great time and plan for the next meeting. Provide space for her to respond. If she turns you down, you shouldn't assume she's just being "hard to get." Please do not try to go out of your way to contact her or accidentally run into her. Respect her boundaries; if she stops talking to you, do not bother her again.

**Here are Some Additional Tips:**

**Keep Good Grooming Habits**

Maintaining good hygiene is a key element in presenting yourself well. This involves several steps, such as:

1. Maintain a clean, shaven appearance or trim your facial hair.
2. Get clean before you go out on a date.
3. Wear Deodorant or antiperspirant, whichever you have chosen.
4. Cologne is optional, but consider smelling nice.
5. Be sure to brush and floss regularly, especially before the date.
6. You should always wear freshly washed and clean clothes.

## Putting Your Best Foot Forward

Keep your body language upbeat and confident. Avoid engaging in these things:

1. Being slouched. Focus on your posture, even if you normally don't.
2. Arms crossed. It's clear that you're taking a defensive stance.
3. Keep non-verbal communication in mind.
4. Avoid restless hand movement. Don't fiddle with your hands or stuff them in your pockets. You want to keep non-verbal communication open and receptive.

### Act Assured, But Be Considerate

1. You must avoid giving off an air of superiority.
2. You don't want her to feel like you're above her.
3. Make yourselves equals in your conversations.
4. If you brag or boast about yourself, she or her friends can become annoyed or turned off by your presence.
5. Don't make a show out of asking her out. Just be yourself.
6. Make it a point to ask about herself, her interest, and her perspective. Understanding her is well-advised.

## Life Skill #92: Planning a Date

Almost everyone fantasizes about going on their ideal date. There are a plethora of date ideas that will work well regardless of whether your date is the romantic, fun-loving type, the adventurous type, or the eccentric, artistic type. Organizing the perfect date takes time and effort, but the fun you'll have is well worth it.

**Make Plans for a Fun Outing. Go to a Standard Date Spot, Like One of These:**

1. Take a tour of your city like a visitor.
2. See a movie—buy tickets.

3. Consider going to a live performance.

4. Attend a sporting event.

5. Visit a cafe, food truck, restaurant, or ice cream shop.

6. Visit a carnival or amusement park.

## Plan an Adventure. A Few Suggestions:

1. Take a trip to the amusement park and thrill ride.

2. You should visit a water park and ride the slides.

3. Participate in an extreme activity in a pair. Activities like skiing, snowboarding, surfing, kayaking, scuba diving, rappelling, and caving are all fantastic.

4. Take your bikes or rent some and head out on the bike trail.

5. Do something neither of you has ever done before, like taking a class in curling, tango, improvised theater, Mongolian cooking, or learning to play a new instrument.

## Make It As Romantic As Possible. Test Out One of These:

1. Take a stroll by the water's edge, be it a river, lake, or pond.

2. Stroll along a historic district street, ideally one with cafés, ice cream parlors, and quaint shops where you can exchange sweet tokens of affection.

3. Make plans to see a play.

**Date Safely**

1. Arrange to meet in a public area, such as a restaurant, cinema, state fair, nightclub, ice rink, concert hall, or comedy club.

2. Be able to get around town without depending on the other person.

3. Have your cash on hand, even if you don't think you'll need it. You could need some extra cash for cab fare or to help with unexpected bills.

# Life Skill #93: Asking a Girl to Be Your Girlfriend

If you have been dating someone for a while, spent enough time together to discuss your expectations for the future, and are ready to commit to a long-term relationship but feel nervous about it...here are some preparations that can help you prepare and get it done smoothly.

**First, Choose the Right Moment.** Pick a comfortable, private setting for your conversation. A moment where you both feel emotionally connected and at ease is ideal. You can take her out on a romantic date if you want to make it memorable. If you're going to do something unique together, you can take her to see the stars, visit an art gallery, go rock climbing, or order her favorite meal. You can give her something small, thoughtful, memorable, long-lasting, such as a jewelry trinket box or a charming keychain. If you'd like to keep things subtle, you can get her a lovely cupcake with a question mark inscribed in the icing.

**Consider Writing a Love Letter.** The written expression of love is a lovely way to tell her how much you care about her and how far you would go to make her happy. Or have a conversation and say how you feel. Be honest and straightforward about your emotions. Make her feel special by sharing your feelings for her, the impact she has on your life, and your hopes for the future of your relationship as you ask her to be your girlfriend. Be patient, give your date time to respond and respect her decision, whether yes or no.

## Life Skill #94: Balancing Time Between Girlfriend and Guy Friends

Especially in the early days of a relationship, when both girlfriends are in the "Every waking moment of my life, I just want to look at you" phase, balancing time between friends and your significant other might feel like an uphill battle. Making time for your significant other and your closest friends takes work. It's doable, though, with a little effort on both ends. Here are some tips.

**Talk to Your Girlfriends and Friends.** Communication is the key to relationships, so make sure your girlfriend and friends know about your desire to spend time with both. Let them know you value both relationships and want a balance that works for everyone.

**Set Aside Special Days to Dedicate to Certain People.** Recognize that occasionally, one group may require more attention than the other. Prioritizing may be necessary in urgent situations during significant events. Just make sure that it doesn't turn into a regular habit.

**Make Plans with Your Girlfriends and Friends in Advance.** This way, you will allocate your time fairly and avoid last-minute conflicts. Or combine your social circles by arranging group outings. This way, you can spend time with both your girlfriend and friends.

**Remember to Schedule Some Alone Time for Yourself.** It is also essential for self-care and maintaining independence. If you have little time, it's okay to say no to invitations or plans and be honest about needing some downtime.

**Make Sure Everyone is On the Same Page.** It's important to prioritize your girlfriend and friends by building trust and spending quality time with them while they understand that you have other important people in your life.

**Lastly, Check In.** Ensure your girlfriend and friends feel appreciated and valued , and that you're striking the right balance.

## Life Skill #95: Treating Girls with Respect

As teenage boys, we're all learning and growing. And when it comes to the opposite sex, we may not always know the best way to act. However, we must never forget to treat girls with respect. This means valuing their bodies, feelings, and opinions and communicating with them in a way that shows we truly care about their input.

When speaking with girls, making eye contact shows that you're interested in what the other person is saying. This regulation is a sign of respect for both girls and guys. Don't make her uncomfortable by staring directly into her eyes; do your best to maintain eye contact.

Allow her to speak. Pay attention, and don't interrupt the girl you're talking to. Wait for her to finish talking before you reply to her. Doing so guarantees that your reply is pertinent and valuable to the discussion at hand.

It's essential to be mindful of how you treat girls. Avoid using vulgar language or behavior, and the Golden Rule's "Treat others as you would like to be treated," especially for girls. Take a moment to reflect on your feelings toward girls and check your prejudices.

Mind your manners and avoid engaging in behavior that can be seen as rude or inappropriate. Don't be a chronic cusser or fart noisemaker. Although you should avoid doing these things in the presence of anyone, girls are typically less amused by them than boys. Sometimes, you might accidentally burp after dinner, and that's fine. Just excuse yourself and carry on.

Never touch anyone, including girls, without first asking their permission. No one is excluded from having the option to offer or withdraw consent to physical touch; this rule is universal. However, the objectification of girl's bodies has received increased attention in the 21st century. Recognize her autonomy by allowing her to control who touches her and when.

Take "no" as the absolute final answer. You should never touch a female without asking for her permission. Many individuals think a girl's reluctance to be touched depends on extraneous circumstances. False. "No" always and completely means "no."

Avoid making comments that could hurt how she feels about her body image. To degrade one girl by making a comparison to another girl's body is rude and inappropriate. It can be seen as a reference to the listener's physique, even if she is not the intended target.

## Life Skill #96: Making a Girl Feel Safe Emotionally and Physically

Establishing a secure emotional environment is a prerequisite for developing lasting girl friendships. Creating a stable relationship by giving the woman in your life your undivided love, safety, and respect. You may already perform some of these activities on a daily basis without even realizing it. If you want to have a happy, healthy relationship with your significant other that can last a lifetime, consider the following tips:

**Take Some One-On-One Time With Her**. Spend time with her to make her feel valued. Getting caught up in your daily routine of studying and other commitments is easy. Plan alone time with your significant other into your busy week. That way, she will never wonder if you truly value her or if she has a place in your heart.

**Pay Close Attention to What She Has to Say.** Engaging in attentive listening demonstrates that you value your girlfriend's opinion. Turn off the TV and put away your phone when conversing with your girlfriend, even if it's just about anything dull. Show your comprehension by nodding, and ask questions if you still don't get anything.

**Be Honest With Her.** To keep her trusting you and feeling safe, never raise her suspicions. You can make a woman feel completely secure in your relationship by always being open and honest with her. Don't lie to her, even if it's a little white lie, so she's never uneasy.

**Open Up to Her.** Exposing yourself as weak demonstrates your trust in her. Relax and be yourself with her as you get to know her more. She'll feel more comfortable doing the same if you're honest and open.

**Show Her Gratitude for What She's Done by Thanking Her.** Ensure your girlfriend knows how much she means to you by telling her how grateful you are for everything she does. Recognize her efforts on your behalf.

## Life Skill #97: Making Your Girl Feel Special

The girl in your life should feel cherished and valued each day. Make sure you tell her daily that you love and appreciate her being in your life. One of the biggest concerns for most guys is whether or not their girlfriend feels appreciated. To help you win her heart, here are a few simple actions you can take.

**Compliment Her Often.** Think of something she hasn't heard before and express your admiration for her beauty, style, personality, or talents. Her self-esteem will increase since she will feel unique and cherished.

**Always Show Her Respect.** Give her total leeway in expressing herself, and fully support her decisions. Understand her desires and respect them without compromising yours. You can discover a lot about your girlfriend and make her feel cared for if you respect her wants without compromising your own.

**Write Her Romantic Love Letters.** Sending your girlfriend a handwritten love note would demonstrate your sincere feelings for her. Writing your sweetheart a letter expressing your feelings about her and your relationship is a terrific way to show that you care.

**Be There for Her.** Make your girlfriend feel loved by being there for her when she is feeling down and out. Help her as much as possible by relieving her suffering, calming her nerves, and giving her confidence and strength to push through tough times.

**Don't Compare Her with Other Girls.** It can end badly if you compare your girl to other ladies. Don't ever do it because it will severely damage your connection with the other person. Don't mention your friend or your sisters as examples of women to compare her to. Each person is unique, and comparisons can be hurtful.

**Listen To Her.** If your girlfriend complains to you about something, take it as a sign that they trust you enough to tell you how they really feel.

**Be Affectionate.** Girls adore public displays of affection like holding hands, short kisses, and arm-draping. Discuss with her how much public expression of love she is comfortable with to make her feel at ease.

**Begin and End Your Day with Her.** Send her a quick text when you wake up and again before you go to sleep, even if you can't see each other every day. This will show her that she is the only person on her mind at the beginning and end of each day.

## Life Skill #98: Interacting With Your Girl's Parents

If you're meeting your girlfriend's parents for the first or second time, it can be awkward to know what to do. You should treat their daughter with respect and interest and show that you love her company. That's what will ultimately matter more to them than your appearance or financial status. But being well-groomed and polite never hurt anyone.

**Talk to Your Girlfriend to Find Out More About Her Family.** Connect with your girlfriend by inquiring about her interests, hobbies, and occupation. Sharing a common interest, like a sports team or a mother's profession, can be a great icebreaker.

**Dress Well.** You should dress appropriately for the event, whether it's a BBQ in jeans and a polo or a formal dinner in trousers and a button-down. You can count on a terrific first impression from this.

**Making a Great First Impression is Essential.** Show your consideration by bringing a small, thoughtful gift. This demonstrates your willingness to make an effort and shows that you care. Don't just arrive empty-handed. Make a statement with a small token of appreciation. You can easily find out what your girlfriend likes by asking her. Remember, it's the little things that make all the difference.

**Keep Your Body Language Upbeat.** Make eye contact, use gestures, and avoid fidgeting to appear friendly and interested. Keep your head up high, create direct eye contact, and avoid slouching.

**Give a Hand or Offer to Clean Up.** To show gratitude to her parents, you should offer to lend a hand. To help clean up, you may assist your girlfriend's dad at the grill or her mother with the dishes. They probably won't need your assistance, but asking never hurts anyone.

**Let Them Know How Much You Appreciate Their Daughter.** Subtly complimenting, showing affection, and talking about her successes or activities will go a long way toward telling parents that you are interested in and appreciate their daughter.

**Be as Mature as You Can.** Communicate gracefully and kindly, using proper etiquette, and avoiding foul language. Show your maturity by discussing your intentions for the future, showing deference to your loved ones. Refrain from moaning or complaining, and avoiding comments that portray you as ignorant.

**Have Good Manners.** Show politeness by not interrupting others, saying "please" and "thank you" appropriately, asking for food, and pulling out a chair for your girlfriend.

**Give Sincere Compliments.** If you want to make a good impression on your girlfriend's parents and show how much you appreciate them, offering sincere compliments is a simple yet effective gesture. They'll appreciate your effort, no matter how big or small the praise is.

**Be Honest.** Your girlfriend's parents will respect and admire you more if you are honest with them about important life choices like where you want to go to college or work.

## Life Skill #99: Maintaining a Healthy Relationship

Maintaining a healthy dating relationship requires effort and commitment from both partners. It is something that can be taught and improved upon over time. Here are some essential tips to help you build and strengthen your connection with your partner.

**Maintain a Level Head**. There is no such thing as a perfect person. To have a healthy connection, one must accept others without trying to change them.

**Communicate With One Another.** Having open lines of communication is crucial for any relationship to thrive. Express your thoughts, feelings, and concerns with your partner while paying close attention to her point of view.

**Respect Boundaries.** Everyone has personal limitations. Respect your partner's boundaries, and communicate clearly. Consent and mutual agreement are crucial in relationships.

**Quality Time.** Spend quality time together to nurture your connection. Plan meaningful dates, engage in shared activities, and create lasting memories.

**Independence.** While spending time together is essential, maintaining individuality is equally vital. Have your interests, hobbies, and friendships balanced to ensure a healthy balance.

**Trust.** The basis of a solid relationship is trust. Be dependable, keep your promises, and avoid behaviors that can damage trust, such as lying or jealousy.

**Conflict Resolution.** Disagreements are natural. Learn to resolve conflicts calmly and respectfully. Focus on the issue at hand, not on blaming each other.

**Appreciation and Affection:** Show appreciation regularly. Small gestures, compliments, and physical affection can strengthen your bond.

**Support.** Be there for each other in times of need. Offer emotional support, encouragement, and understanding during challenges.

**Intimacy.** Emotional and physical connections are vital. Make sure both partners feel comfortable with this aspect of the relationship.

**Future Planning**. Discuss your long- term goals and aspirations. Understanding each other's plans can help you align your paths and build a future together if that's your mutual desire.

**Forgiveness.** Holding on to grudges can be toxic. Learn to forgive and move forward when mistakes are made. No one is perfect, and forgiveness can strengthen your bond.

**Be Flexible.** It's normal to have some apprehension about new situations. Positive interactions pave the way for development and progress.

**Seek Help When Needed.** If you encounter persistent issues or feel overwhelmed, consider seeking professional help or relationship counseling.

## Life Skill #100: Breaking Up Respectfully

Some of the things you may miss after a split include your ex's family and the support and solace you shared at a difficult time. Maybe you're worried about hurting the other person's feelings, or you don't want to make a terrible impression in front of your friends. The point is that ending a relationship is never pleasant, even if necessary.

### Breakup Dos and Don'ts

**Dos:**

- Consider how you feel and why you're making this choice. Do what you know is right, even if it causes someone else pain. Be mindful of how you say it.

- Being considerate and ready for a response requires putting yourself in the other person's shoes. How will you respond, for instance, if the person you're breaking up with is emotional or angry? This might make you more wise and ready for anything.

- Have good intentions. Demonstrate your care for others by treating them with kindness, honesty, sensitivity, respect, and care.

- Be honest but not brutal. The most crucial points are that you should be kind and compassionate while still being honest and not equate honesty with harshness. When explaining why something isn't working, avoid criticizing the other person.

- Say it in person. Breaking up in person is the most respectful and empathetic way to end a relationship. Think about how you would feel if your boyfriend or girlfriend ignored you via text or social media.

- If you feel more comfortable talking to someone, do so. Having a trusted buddy to vent to can be helpful during a breakup, but only if that friend keeps your communication private until after the breakup. Adults like parents, elder siblings, and friends are good people to confide in since they are less likely to gossip or make the information  inadvertently public.

**Don't:**

- It can make things more difficult in the long term if you avoid conversing with the person you're breaking up with. Putting things off also increases the likelihood that the person will hear the news from someone other than you.
- Rush through the process and plunge right into a complex topic.
- Be disrespectful. Avoid negative comments and gossip while discussing your ex. Imagine how it would feel if your ex spoke highly of you after you two broke up.

# Chapter 11

## Communicating and Being a Good Person

Lucas knew he wasn't a good communicator. When things got tough, he shut down, often muttering his frustration to himself in hopes that the walls would magically understand. But in a world where effective communication is a vital life skill, Lucas wasn't alone in his struggles. Let's explore the art of communication from various angles.

## Life Skill #101: Learning to Listen

Regardless of the nature of the discourse, listen attentively is a crucial skill. It aids in establishing rapport, facilitating understanding, settling disputes, and increasing precision. If you want to improve your listening skills, consider these seven easy steps:

**Step 1: Create a Setting Where It is Easy to Discuss**

Help someone who is having difficulty communicating by facilitating a deep conversation. You can strike up a conversation with them over cafe', a meal, or a baseball game. Provide them with the opportunity to respond.

**Step 2: Talk Less, Listen More**

Being fully present and focused on what they're saying is essential when conversing with someone. Concentrate on the present moment and pay attention to what the other person is saying rather than letting your thoughts wander. Remember, it's not just about what you have to say--giving the other person space to talk and genuinely listening to them is just as important, if not more so.

**Step 3: Be Okay with Silence**

Silences in conversations may seem uncomfortable, but they can be beneficial. They provide an opportunity for reflection and understanding. Experts suggest that waiting silently for a response from the person you're speaking with can lead to a better grasp of the conversation. Some of life's most essential discussions only require a little talking.

**Step 4: Ask good Questions**

Show that you're paying attention by asking clarifying questions. Ask a question similar to what they just said, or inquire about the details you missed. Both forms of active listening demonstrate comprehension and give the person being listened to a sense of worth.

## Step 5: Be Cautious about Revealing Private Information

While speaking from personal experience can strengthen bonds, it shouldn't be used to offer solutions or take control of the conversation. Avoid making the talk about yourself and instead prioritize their needs in the conversation.

## Step 6:. Don't Worry If You Can't Find the Appropriate Words

We shouldn't stress about saying the perfect thing or being the hero in talks. Instead, we should focus on being there, listening, and participating. Being heard and validated is more helpful to the other person than advice. Listening to someone is only the first step in developing a meaningful connection.

## Step 7: Acknowledge Their Vulnerability

Recognizing the other person's openness and expressing gratitude for their trust, you can pave the way for more communication. Consider having a tough talk as the first step towards providing assistance.

# Life Skill #102: Nailing Communication

Communication isn't just about the words you say, it's about how you say them and what your body is saying without words. The tone of voice, facial expressions, and body language all play important roles in conveying and understanding messages. To enhance your communication skills, check out the following:

**Keep It Clear and Simple**

When you talk, use words everyone understands, and keep everything simple. Avoid complex language, unnecessary jargon, and repetition. People tune out when you repeat yourself a million times.

**Prepare Ahead of Time**

Before you start talking, know your stuff. Research the information you'll need to back up your message so you're ready for any questions or objections. Prepare yourself to talk about a variety of topics and provide justification for your perspective. It's like being a champ in a video game. You have to be prepared for the boss level.

## Pay Attention to Your Vibe

Be mindful of your nonverbal cues. Ensure that your body language and facial expressions align with your spoken words. Inconsistency confuses people.

## Tone Matters

Pay attention to your tone. A misjudged tone can escalate conflicts. Adjust your tone as necessary during conversations. Along with loudness, projection, and tone, vocal variety also includes word choice. Awareness of your tone while you speak will allow you to adjust it as needed. Reading texts and emails multiple times and waiting a day or two before responding can help maintain a neutral tone. You may find it easier to digest if you reread the message once your emotions have settled.

## Practice Active Listening

It's not just about talking. It's about listening too. Passive listening causes you to miss 50% of what the other person says. Give your full attention, ask questions for clarification, and provide feedback to enhance understanding. You will learn more when you listen.

## Build Your Emotional Intelligence

Effective communication depends on your ability to recognize your feelings. Understanding the other person's perspective or where others are coming from can help you prevent misunderstandings and soothe damaged sentiments.

**Plan Your Chat**

When you have something important to say, plan it out. Think about the timing, who you're talking to, and the best way to deliver your message. By planning, you can ensure everyone who needs to know important information is informed.

**Create a Positive Vibe**

Trust and positive energy are vital in any group. Go for the laid-back, sympathetic, and open type of guy. Everyone wants you on their team if you can effectively communicate.

# Life Skill #103: Reading Body Language

Reading nonverbal cues is one of the most useful skills one can learn. Here are some great pointers to help you understand the body language of others around you.

**Study the Eyes**

Eyes reveal a lot. A person's eye behavior can infer expressions of boredom, disinterest, or dishonesty, making it an integral aspect of communication. An increased blinking rate may imply deception, while dilated pupils may signal a positive response. As a general rule, looking longingly at something suggests an interest in it, while looking up and to the right during the discussion is a sign of lying, and looking up to the left is a sign of telling the truth.

## Gaze at the Face

Facial expressions can also reveal a lot about a person. Smiling uses the entire face instead of a fake grin using only the mouth. While tense lips convey dissatisfaction, loose ones indicate happiness. Touching one's lips or covering one's mouth while speaking might indicate dishonesty.

## Pay Attention to the Proximity

Your closeness to another person can tell you much about your relationship. If the other person backs away or walks away as you approach, it can be a sign of unease. Remember that this can vary because various cultures have different expectations of personal space.

## Check to See Whether Your Partner is Mimicking Your Actions

Mirroring involves taking on the other person's posture and gestures. Look to see if the person you're talking to is doing anything you're doing, such as leaning an elbow on the table or sipping from a glass. If they do,they want to get to know you better.

**Observe the Head Movement**

Nodding indicates patience. Tilting the head sideways or backward shows interest, and pointing with the head or face is a sign of interest. People with power are often looked at more often than less-significant people.

**Watch the Feet**

Because most people spend most of their attention on their faces and upper bodies, their feet typically carry an unspoken message. A person's foot movement can reveal how they feel about you. Their feet pointing in your direction usually indicate that they are interested in you. If their feet point away, they may not want to give you their full attention.

**Monitor Hand Signals**

Notice if they put their hands in their pockets when they are standing. Keep an eye out for hand signals like putting hands on the head or putting hands in pockets. The use of an elbow as a headrest indicates either attentiveness or boredom.

Holding an object between two people is called a blocking act in nonverbal communication.

**Take a Look at How the Arm's Position**

Positioning one's hands on one's hips is a dominant gesture, whereas crossing one's arms can convey defensiveness, nervousness, vulnerability, or a lack of openness.

## Life Skill #104: Having Empathy

It takes empathy to get along with people. It's not a talent you're born with but a skill you can improve. People with high empathy are well-liked and successful in many areas of life. However, narcissism and antisocial personality disorder are two of the many personality disorders linked to a reduced capacity for empathy. Though it may seem impossible at first, becoming more empathic is a skill that can be honed with time and effort.

- **Get Interested In Unknown Individuals**. People who are empathetic are individuals who genuinely want to learn more about others. They may approach strangers for a chat or watch others without bias. They have maintained the childlike sense of wonder that exists in all of us. Curiosity increases our capacity for empathy by introducing us to people, places, and things that would otherwise be out of reach.

- **Focus On Similarities**. Everyone tends to hold certain beliefs and experiences. Avoid making hasty judgments based on differences. Instead, seek common ground with others. You can better connect with them and understand their viewpoints by finding similarities.

- **Try to See Things From Their Point of View.** The best way to develop empathy is to put yourself in someone else's shoes. When you encounter someone with a different background or situation, take a moment to imagine life from their point of view. For instance, if you see a homeless person at the railway station, take a moment to learn about their situation and consider how you can help rather than dismiss them because of how they seem. Volunteering at a local soup kitchen or simply delivering food or a care package with a friendly greeting are all good options.

- **Listen, But Also Share.** Understanding the feelings of others is only part of what it means to be empathetic. Developing genuine empathy for another person is only possible if you trust them with your innermost thoughts and emotions. The wonderful thing about empathy is that it works both ways.

- **Participate In Social Action Groups.** The concept of empathy can be applied to more than just oneself. Its reach and scope can include communities and even the world. One way to show compassion is to join a support group or volunteer for a good cause.

- **Get Creative With It**. Understanding others can be challenging, mainly if their belief or lifestyle differ. When empathizing feels difficult or unattainable, using your imagination and creativity is crucial. You can try to picture how they feel, even in tricky situations. Your creativity might surprise you with new insights and ways to connect.

## Life Skill #105: Being a Stand-Up Guy

Being compassionate person isn't just for grown-up, it's the ability that may make you a legend among your peers. It's all about understanding someone's feelings and doing your best to brighten their day. Yet not everybody is comfortable displaying it. If you wonder how to be the hero of your own story, read on.

**Lend a Helping Hand**

You know how it feels when you're stuck on a difficult video game level and a friend steps in to assist. That is the kind of kindness we are discussing. Offer to help a friend with homework or at a game. Or go grocery shopping for a neighbor. Even small act of kindness, like holding the door or picking up something somebody dropped, can have a significant impact.

## Respect the No

Respect is like a secret code among friends. When someone says "no" or "I don't want to," it's important to listen. If your buddy isn't up for hanging out or sharing their stuff, don't push. Give them space, and they will appreciate it.

## Offer Hope

You never know when your words can be a lifeline for someone. Let's say your friend is having a tough time, like losing a loved one. Here's where you step in. Tell them they're strong, that they got this. Your word of encouragement can make all the difference.

## Be Their Biggest Cheerleader

Imagine your friend is trying out for the school basketball team. Let them know you believe in them. Encourage them to keep going, even when they feel like giving up. Your support can be the wind beneath their wings.

## Validate Their Feelings

One way to express your concern is to acknowledge their feelings. Sometimes, saying, "I get it, you're having a tough day," can mean the world to someone. It shows that you care about what they're going though. So, when a friend is down, be there to listen. You don't have to have all the answer, just an open ear, and sometimes, people just need to be heard.

## Forgive Them

You know how you mess up in a game now and then. People make mistakes, too. When someone says sorry and means it, be cool about it. Forgiving is like hitting the reset button of a friendship. It lets you start fresh.

# Life Skill #106: Reading Situations

To succeed in our careers (and in life), situational awareness is one of the most valuable skills you can have. It's all about picking up on the little details that aren't always said outright, like body language, tone of voice, hidden messages, and people's intentions. These things aren't always obvious and takes a lot of practice and training to read them correctly.

**Practice. Practice. Practice.**

First things first, there's no magic to this. It's all about practice; in sports or learning an instrument. Reading situation is a skill you can develop, not an innate one. The best way to learn is to stop thinking about learning and start doing; stop overthinking and actively dive in .

**Understand the Big Picture**

Before diving in, take a moment to understand what's going on.

- Where exactly are you stepping foot?
- Who are the players, exactly?
- Who else is involved, and what do they want to get out of this?
- What do other people hope to accomplish?
- What did you do to get where you are now?
- Where do you fit into this, if at all?

Understanding the bigger picture is crucial for deciphering the smaller pieces.

**Make People a Priority**

People are complex and challenging to read, so learning to do so calls for curiosity, patience, and compassion.

## Hear What is Being Said. And What Is Not.

Pay close attention to what the folks are saying, but also pay attention to their tone, subtext, and facial expressions, and then probe with insightful questions to learn more.

## Get Feedback

Feedback is your friend. Seek it out, listen to it, and use it to improve. It's like having a cheat code for progress. So get input in as many ways as possible.

## Try Imagining the World Through the Other Person's Eyes

A better reader must have empathy and curiosity for the other person in order to comprehend their thoughts, feelings, and goals.

## Leave Your Assumptions Behind

Keep an open mind. Avoid letting your biases, preconceptions, absolutes, and assumptions cloud your judgment as you try to understand a new circumstance. Stop projecting your ideas onto the situation and attempt to perceive it as it is.

## Embrace Failure

It's okay to make mistake, they help you improve. Even the best gamers lose sometimes, but that's how they learn and get even better.

## Life Skill #107: Trusting Your Gut

Intuition is like your inner wisdom, a superpower passed down through time. But it's not enough to feel it. It takes additional thought and reason to act on it. We're all trying to be as savvy as possible in every situation. You can get better at trusting your instincts with practice and careful thinking. Here's how to tune into your inner wisdom.

**Listen to Your First Reaction**

Your gut feeling isn't just some random emotion. It's your brain quickly analyzing everything it knows. So pay attention to your first thoughts when facing a decision or problem.

**Distinguish Gut Feelings From Bias**

Sometimes our gut feelings can be influenced by our personal biases. Like when you're watching a game, you want your team to win just because you love them. Try to separate facts from feelings.

**Practice Makes Perfect**

Practice makes your instincts sharper. Try out low-risk situations. What does your gut tell you? Which sense do you use first? This method helps with exercising and validating your gut feelings. Use it like a trusty sidekick to make everyday choices.

**Score Your Gut**

Stop and ask yourself how you would rate your first reaction. Make a mental note of how your gut instinct saved the day or led you to a terrific outcome. When making a snap decision under pressure, trust your instincts but pay close attention to the details to arrive at a reasonable conclusion.

# Life Skill #108: Advocating for Yourself

It's crucial to understand what matters most to you in life. Being able to advocate for yourself, standing up for your rights, and recognizing your limitations are significant skills. Knowing who to approach for help and how to ask for it is also essential. It's all about learning how to express yourself assertively, and here are some helpful tips and guidelines to help you achieve that.

**Prioritize You**

Your needs matter most. To be a great advocate, believe in yourself, and know what you need and want. It's all about you.

## Know Your Rights

You've got rights. Check out the rules and regulations that affect you. There's a world of trustworthy resources like the internet, books, workshops, and community and peer-based organizations.

## Keep Records

Don't rely on your memory. Document everything that can support your case. Keep your paperwork in one organized place. It'll help your self-advocacy efforts.

## Prepare and Plan

Make a plan for your needs now and in the future. Consider what you'll need, review relevant paperwork, and consult reliable sources.

## Clear Communication

Express yourself assertively but respectfully. Be clear and concise in your communication; avoid aggressive or passive language. Keep meetings brief and to the point, and make notes beforehand. Maintain the focus of your discussions and collaborate to find solutions.

## Choose the Right Person

Decide who can best assist you with your particular problem or request. Be professional and considerate when speaking with them.

## Follow Up and Thank Others

After making a request or seeking assistance, follow up on the process. Express gratitude to everybody who has assisted you.

## Advocate and Appeal

You have the legal right to ask a higher court to reconsider your case if it is decided against you. You must file your appeal before the deadline to secure your right to a fair trial and competent representation in court.

# Life Skill #109: Learning to Say No

Learning to say no is a vital life skill and can be challenging. We all have limited time and energy, so it's essential to prioritize our commitments carefully. It's imperative to know when and how to decline a request and why it's preferable to say no rather than yes sometimes. Here's how to say "no" politely and effectively.

## Be Direct

Refrain from evading the question or giving flimsy justifications. The only thing this does is give the other person a chance to respond. Don't hesitate or put things off. When you want to say "no," just say it. A simple and direct "no" works the best. If it's necessary, give a quick explanation, but do just what is needed.

## Polite Assertiveness

Be polite but firm . For example, you can say, "I'm afraid I can't help at the moment, but I'll be sure to let you know if things change." Or try, "I appreciate you asking, but I've got a pretty busy schedule."

## Understand People's Tactics

Sometimes, people might use tricks to get you to say yes, especially when asking for money or favors. Some people and groups resort to manipulative strategies like "forced options" and "social pressure" to get what they want. Someone might mention that others are giving X dollars, $20, $30, etc. How much do you want to give, then? Stick to your decision to say no.

## Set Boundaries

It's important to know your limits in relationships and commitments. When you understand your role in them, it's easier to say "no" without feeling guilty.

## Negotiate

In professional situations, like at work, you can negotiate, and it's super effective. Imagine your boss giving you a big task that feels overwhelming. You can suggest a different approach that suits you better. For instance, you might say, "I can handle tasks X, Y, and Z, but to do them well, it'll take me three weeks instead of two. How would you like me to prioritize them?"

## Stay Firm

Real friends and respectful people will get it if you say no. Don't give in to pressure. Stay firm and calm. If someone can't accept your request, it's a sign they might not be a true friend or may not respect you. Don't give in just because they feel uncomfortable.

## Think About You

Remember, taking care of yourself isn't selfish. Successful people say no to many things to focus on what really matters. Saying no is a way to look after yourself and your goals.

# Life Skill #110: Practicing Humility

Humility is a difficult trait to develop. It's all about being down-to-earth and accepting yourself and others. It can be challenging, especially when you're doing well in life. It is easier to stay humble when you start, but as you grow and you're the top, people look up to you for guidance. Be careful. You could become arrogant and conceited once you reach to the top. Here are some exercises to practice staying humble.

## Spend Time Listening to Others

Being humble means listening to others and respecting their opinions. Try active listening, where you pay attention when someone's talking. Give them space to share.

## Stay Present

Practicing humbleness involves accepting yourself, flaws, and all. Mindfulness emphasizes being present without judgment, and kindness toward to yourself is crucial for improvement.

## Be Grateful for What You Have

Stop and think about how fortunate you are. Wanting more of yourself or other things can be a self-destructive cycle. Practice gratitude can help you appreciate what you've got and stay humble and optimistic.

## Ask for Help When You Need It

It's okay to seek help when needed it, and it's a sign of strength, not weakness. Sometimes, we might feel a sense of pride in solving our problems independently, but recognizing our limits and reaching out for assistance is an actual display of humility. It shows that you're aware of your incapabilities and are open to learning and growing with the support of others.

## Seek Other's Opinions

Whether you are in charge or not, it's essential to value other's input. Encourage people to share their thoughts, even anonymously, if necessary. Be open to constructive criticism and show appreciation for it.

## Check Your Ego

Pride and arrogance are not-so-great feelings because they make us all smug and snobby. It's not always easy to keep these feelings in check, especially when we've done something incredible and everyone is patting us on the back. However, we don't usually call this pride or arrogance because it often has a bad reputation.

# Dear Awesome Teens and Supportive Parents!

Completing "110 Life Skills for Teenage Boys" is an outstanding achievement! I hope this journey was as enlightening for you as it was for us creating it. My goal is to equip young minds with essential skills to navigate the challenges of adolescence and beyond. Your feedback is invaluable in shaping future editions and helping more teens benefit from this resource.

Teenagers, your insight are gem! Share your reflections on which life skills inspired you, how they influenced your daily routine, or any ninja moves that save your day.

Parents, we value your perspective too! How did you see these skills impacting your teens? Any "aha" moments or positive changes you observed?

Please take a moment to share your thoughts on Amazon by dropping a review. Your opinions are important to me, and I appreciate your time and contribution to the community.

Thank you for being part of this journey towards empowering the next generation with crucial life skills.

Warm regards,

Tory Hunt

# Conclusion

Your teenage years are an incredible journey filled with changes, challenges, and growth. It's time to start wondering about the practical stuff in life that often gets overlooked in school. You might be thinking about managing money, doing laundry, or even maintaining a car. It's perfectly normal to have these questions and uncertainties.

But guess what? You're not alone in this. Many young people like you wish they had more guidance on these essential life skills. A lot of recent graduates feel the same way. So don't worry if you're finding it overwhelming. You're on the right track by seeking knowledge and preparing for life's adventures.

This guide has provided valuable insights and practical advice on various aspects of life, from school to finance to family. Take your time to go through each chapter, take notes, and use it as your handbook for growing up.

In the next few years, you'll discover more about yourself, your values, and your life goals. This knowledge will inspire you to embark on exciting and unforgettable adventures that shape your life. Remember, this isn't about being perfect. It's about getting better, growing, and becoming the best version of yourself. You might stumble sometimes, but that's all part of the adventure. These skills will help you stand up and keep moving forward.

So start with the first chapter and focus on taking care of yourself. You're on your way to becoming a confident, capable young adult. Let's do this.

# Reference

A Routine Car Maintenance Schedule Based on Engine Mileage. (2012). CarsDirect. https://www.carsdirect.com/car-maintenance/a-routine-car-maintenance-schedule-based-on-engine-mileage

American Red Cross. (2019). *CPR Steps*. Red Cross. https://www.redcross.org/take-a-class/cpr/performing-cpr/cpr-steps

Bliss, S. (n.d.). 9 Ways To Find Your Perfect Career Match. Forbes. Retrieved June 20, 2023, from https://www.forbes.com/sites/sarabliss/2019/04/29/9-ways-to-find-your-perfect-career-match/?sh=4e89c31aec75

Cherry, K. (2017). *Understanding Body Language and Facial Expressions*. Verywell Mind; Verywellmind. https://www.verywellmind.com/understand-body-language-and-facial-expressions-4147228

c) Copyright skillsyouneed.com 2011-2019. (2011). *Humility | SkillsYouNeed*. Skillsyouneed.com. https://www.skillsyouneed.com/ps/humility.html

Contributor, G. (2019, April 6). *How to Back Up a Trailer...Like a Man!* The Art of Manliness. https://www.artofmanliness.com/skills/manly-know-how/how-to-back-up-a-trailer-like-a-man/

Choking: First aid. (n.d.). Mayo Clinic. https://www.mayoclinic.org/first-aid/first-aid-choking/basics/art-20056637#:~:text=Bend%20the%20person%20over%20at

Dale, T. (2022, November 10). How to Turn Off Water to Your House - Advice From Bob Vila. Bob Vila. https://www.bobvila.com/articles/turn-off-water/

Derr, A. (2015, August 14). *How to purify water in the wild.* Scouting Magazine. https://scoutingmagazine.org/2015/08/how-to-purify-water-no-matter-where-you-are/#:~:text=Boiling%20water%20from%20an%20in

Emerson, M. S. (2021, August 30). *Eight Things You Can Do To Improve Your Communication Skills.* Professional Development | Harvard DCE. https://professional.dce.harvard.edu/blog/eight-things-you-can-do-to-improve-your-communication-skills/

Formisano, B. (2021). How to Turn Off Power at the Electrical Service Panel. The Spruce. https://www.thespruce.com/safely-turn-off-power-at-electrical-panel-1824677#:~:text=Carefully%20push%20the%20toggle%20lever,dark%20at%20the%20same%20time

How to Check Your Car's Engine Oil. (n.d.). Consumer Reports. https://www.consumerreports.org/car-repair-maintenance/how-to-check-car-engine-oil-a7618306432/#:~:text=With%20the%20engine%20off%2C%20open

How To Drive a Stick Shift. (2012, March 28). Driving-Tests.org. https://driving-tests.org/beginner-drivers/how-to-drive-a-stick-shift/

How to Ask for a Promotion: A Step-By-Step Guide. (n.d.). Coursera. https://www.coursera.org/articles/how-to-ask-for-a-promotion

How to File Your Federal Taxes | USAGov. (n.d.). Www.usa.gov. https://www.usa.gov/file-taxes

How to Use a Compass | REI Co-op. (n.d.). REI. https://www.rei.com/learn/expert-advice/navigation-basics.html#:~:text=Hold%20your%20compass%20flat%20with

How to pay your taxes | Internal Revenue Service. (n.d.). Www.irs.gov. https://www.irs.gov/newsroom/how-to-pay-your-taxes

How to Identify Poisonous Plants. (n.d.). Be Prepared - Emergency Essentials. https://beprepared.com/blogs/articles/how-to-identify-poisonous-plants

Here's What You'll Need to Start Foraging Mushrooms. (2020, July 13). Wirecutter: Reviews for the Real World. https://www.nytimes.com/wirecutter/blog/how-to-hunt-mushrooms/

How to Hunt: A Step-by-Step Guide for New Adult Hunters. (2020, June 1). Outdoor Life. https://www.outdoorlife.com/story/hunting/how-to-hunt-step-by-step-guide-for-new-adult-hunters/

How to Break Up Respectfully (for Teens) - KidsHealth. (2019). Kidshealth.org. https://kidshealth.org/en/teens/break-up.html

Hogan, L. (2021, August 25). How to Be More Empathetic. WebMD. https://www.webmd.com/balance/features/how-to-be-more-empathetic

How to use a compass. (n.d.). Countryfile.com. Retrieved June 21, 2023, from https://www.countryfile.com/go-outdoors/how-to-use-a-compass/

https://www.howstuffworks.com/about-charles-w-bryant.htm. (2008, January 7). How to Find Water in the Wild. MapQuest Travel. https://www.mapquest.com/travel/survival/wilderness/how-to-find-water.htm

Krans, B. (2014, July 21). Heimlich Maneuver. Healthline; Healthline Media. https://www.healthline.com/health/heimlich-maneuver

Kraft, R. (2018, October 18). *10 WAYS TO HELP READ A SITUATION*. PERSPECTIVE: A FORUM for FILM, TV, and MEDIA COMPOSERS. https://perspectiveforum.net/2018/10/18/10-ways-help-read-situation/

Lipford, D. (2023). How to Use Power Tools. Today's Homeowner. https://todayshomeowner.com/tools/guides/understanding-power-tools/

Lost? Find Directions Without Compass | The Old Farmer's Almanac. (n.d.). Www.almanac.com. https://www.almanac.com/find-your-way-without-compass

McKay, B. & K. (2011, March 29). How to Perform the Fireman's Carry. The Art of Manliness. https://www.artofmanliness.com/skills/manly-know-how/how-to-perform-the-firemans-carry/#:~:text=Grab%20the%20victim

Never settle for less than you deserve. - Unknown - Quotespedia.org. Www.quotespedia.org. Retrieved June 20, 2023, from https://www.quotespedia.org/authors/u/unknown/never-settle-for-less-than-you-deserve-unknown/

Nolo. (2011, October 10). *Police Stops: What to Do If You Are Pulled Over*. Www.nolo.com; Nolo. https://www.nolo.com/legal-encyclopedia/police-stops-when-pulled-over-30186.html

published, R. C. (2022, July 3). *Foraging for berries – where and how to pick them in the wild*. Homesandgardens.com. https://www.homesandgardens.com/gardens/foraging-for-berries

staff, familydoctor org editorial. (2018, March 13). *Deciding When to See a Doctor*. Familydoctor.org. https://familydoctor.org/deciding-see-doctor/

 Should I Call an Ambulance or Drive to the Hospital? | Emergency Medicine. (n.d.). Main Line Health. https://www.mainlinehealth.org/specialties/emergency-medicine/when-to-call-an-ambulance

10 ways to help you boost your retirement savings (whatever your age). (2018). Merrill Edge. https://www.merrilledge.com/article/10-tips-to-help-you-boost-your-retirement-savings-whatever-your-age-ose

Src="https://Secure.gravatar.com/Avatar/B88ae55604aa62c263cb8c25296b8312?s=32, img C., d=mm, H, r=g">Family, Sep. 21, ymanUpdated:, & 2020. (n.d.). *Cut Down a Tree Safely*. Family Handyman. https://www.familyhandyman.com/list/how-to-cut-down-a-tree/

10 Steps to Effective Self-Advocacy - Disability Rights Florida. (n.d.). Disabilityrightsflorida.org. https://disabilityrightsflorida.org/disability-topics/disability_topic_info/10_steps_to_effective_self_advocacy

Suits Expert. (2023, April 8). Men's Suits Guide: How to Choose the Perfect Suit - Suits Expert. https://www.suitsexpert.com/men-suits-guide

Sole, C. (2018). How to Use a Hand Saw. Better Homes & Gardens. https://www.bhg.com/home-improvement/remodeling/carpentry/how-to-use-a-hand-saw/

Tips for a Successful Interview. (2022). University of North Georgia. https://ung.edu/career-services/online-career-resources/interview-well/tips-for-a-successful-interview.php

Top 6 Gritty Ways to Start a Fire in the Wild | Outdoorsy.com. (2023, January 5). Outdoorsy RV Blogs. https://www.outdoorsy.com/blog/top-6-gritty-ways-to-start-a-fire-in-the-wild?wb-auto_radius=true&wb-currency=USD&wb-instant_book=true&wb-locale=en-us&wb-page%5Blimit%5D=4&wb-page%5Boffset%5D=0